P

Living with LEO:
Law Enforcement Officer

Everyone who goes thru the academy should have this book as a training manual for their LEO supporter. There is so much to learn and this is a fast charming book that can help to understand the "quirks" that these wonderful men and women are born with!

—Kathleen Hughes, wife of Timothy Hughes,
Badge #793, Arizona Highway Patrol,
Retired, 22 years of service

An entertaining, yet insightful look into the "better half" of a challenging career. A must read for both the LEO and supporter.

—Dean Faust, Retired Payson Police Detective,
22 years of service

A witty book that brings back so many memories! This book is a must-read for LEO supporters. The author does a great job of showing laugh-out-loud humor on a difficult profession.

—Cathy Boone, wife of Ernie Boone,
Retired Gilbert Police Department, 23 years of service

Monica,
I treasure you
And your entire familes
friendship. Best of Luck.
Donald B. Engler
Chief of Police
Payson Police Department

LIVING WITH
LEO

To Monica,
   Thank you for your
cherished friendship!

      Godspeed &
Very Best Wishes,

   Sherry W Engler

21 July 2018

LIVING WITH
LEO

Law Enforcement Officer

SHERRY ENGLER

TATE PUBLISHING
AND **ENTERPRISES**, LLC

Published by Tate Publishing & Enterprises, LLC
127 E. Trade Center Terrace | Mustang, Oklahoma 73064 USA
1.888.361.9473 | www.tatepublishing.com

Tate Publishing is committed to excellence in the publishing industry. The company reflects the philosophy established by the founders, based on Psalm 68:11,
"The Lord gave the word and great was the company of those who published it."

Book design copyright © 2013 by Tate Publishing, LLC. All rights reserved.
Cover design by Rtor Maghuyop
Interior design by Jake Muelle

Published in the United States of America

ISBN: 978-1-62510-297-3
1. Family & Relationships / Family Relationships
2. Family & Relationships / Marriage
13.07.01

DISCLAIMER

Due to the sensitive nature of certain events depicted in *Living with LEO (Law Enforcement Officer)*, details and descriptions have been changed to protect the anonymity of law enforcement officers, LEO supporters, and involved citizens.

DEDICATION

*L*iving with LEO (Law Enforcement Officer) is dedicated to all the courageous women and men who dedicate their lives supporting the law enforcement officer; and to the brave and fearless law enforcement officers who dedicate their lives to make our world a better and safer place; and to my three LEOs who have been a gift of inspiration and a source of humor in my life.

ACKNOWLEDGMENTS

*L*iving *with LEO (Law Enforcement Officer)* is the product of sharing an unpredictable life with my husband, Don, who through his courage, valor, integrity, and a few quirky traits has been a great source of inspiration to me. To our children, Brandyce and Donald, who have ventured forth in the world of law enforcement, and who have blessed our lives so richly everyday by sharing cherished moments of life; for it is the strength and dedication of these three individuals that will forever remain close to my heart. Thank you to family and friends, and to the men and women in law enforcement who are willing to give the ultimate sacrifice to make our world a safer and better place; and to their supporters, who are able to meet the challenges of living with a law enforcement officer with courage, strength, love, and a large reserve of patience. And especially to the brave and courageous brothers and sisters in law enforcement who gave all. May you forever rest in peace with the Father. And to God, our Father, who gives strength to me and others in the family of law enforcement.

TABLE OF CONTENTS

INTRODUCTION

As the wife of a law enforcement officer for over twenty-eight years, and the mother of a daughter and a son, who both are law enforcement officers, I have experienced what it is like living with a LEO from two different perspectives. While living with LEOs can be rather difficult at times due to some quirky behaviors they may acquire, they are rather humorous creatures. I find life is much richer laughing at the peculiar things LEOs may do rather than crying over the difficulties associated with law enforcement, a consistency of inconsistencies.

The LEO supporter faces many hurdles. Many of the hurdles may be life-changing experiences. LEO supporters are gifted beings who are very patient, understanding, and have the ability to row with the flow in the constantly changing unpredictable waters of law enforcement. As the LEO faces many challenges in the criminal world, so too does the LEO supporter. With great strength of character and many, many prayers, the LEO supporter will survive.

I invite you to read about the three LEOs with whom I share life and compare them to your LEO. I am sure some of these quick read chapters will seem familiar to you, as you identify with similar, interesting traits your LEO displays. May you laugh; may you ponder the similarities; may you think of your LEO in a humorous light. But, may you always pray. Pray for LEO's safety; pray for yours. Pray for peace; pray for serenity; pray for the gift of life; pray for a better world; for it is through prayers we gain the strength necessary to be able to laugh instead of cry.

ARE YOU NORMAL?

If you are currently living with a law enforcement officer (LEO), you probably have guessed that LEOs are not normal creatures. So you may ask yourself if you are abnormal by association.

For example, one morning you hear a continuous click. *Click, click, click. Click, click, click.* Over and over. It is three o'clock in the morning, so you sleepily drag your body out of bed to see what the clicking is all about. There he stands in the living room, your LEO, in his underwear holding his duty weapon in his shooting stance, pointing his Glock toward the window, "dry-firing" his gun over and over. *Click, click, click.*

You ask, "What are you doing, hon?"

LEO answers, "We have to qualify today, so I thought I would get in a little practice dry-firing."

You sleepily answer, "Okay, I think I'm going back to bed."

Click, click, click. "Okay," your LEO says.

This is really not what other normal mainstream people do. Most other normal persons are tucked snuggly away in bed and do not dry-fire a weapon at three in the morning or witness someone else doing so.

LEOs are very loveable creatures; they are just very different. And to live with one, it takes some courage, some understanding (to say the least), and the ability to adapt to their abnormal behaviors.

The funny part is if you tell this story to other LEOs, they can totally relate to "dry-firing" at 3:00 a.m. After all, qualifying with their duty weapon is one of the most important aspects of keeping them alive on the job. "What is so strange about it?" they may ask, seeming not to comprehend why anyone would ever think this is a strange behavior.

Society on a whole understands that LEOs (law enforcement officers) are very different in nature. Society is intrigued with them. There are numerous television shows depicting cops, in reality and in fiction. There are numerous books written by psychologists and even fellow "warriors" about the professional law enforcement officer. But to truly see the difference between a LEO and a normal person is to live with one, which isn't always the easiest.

All law enforcement officers share common bonds; strong common bonds such as integrity, bravery, honor, and valor to name a few. They also share a common goal: to make this world a safe place by taking down the bad guys while trying to keep themselves out of harm's way in the process.

If you truly think about their profession, it is an enormous challenge and sometimes at an enormous expense—their lives. So it is easy to see why LEO may be dry-firing—*click, click, click*—in the early morning hours. It is just living with LEO, dry-firing at 3:00 a.m. that takes an enormous amount of patience.

TINY TOTS, BIG HEARTS, AND THE DREAM

Not everyone can be a law enforcement officer (LEO). Just like Superman, the individuals who become LEOs have a special makeup the rest of us don't. If you live with a LEO, you should know that we too have a special makeup others don't—*patience* and the ability to live down the overwhelming urge to commit homicide on occasions.

If you think finding your LEO in his underwear, dry-firing his weapon is somewhat on the inconvenient side, this is probably one of the least inconvenient things LEO may do. So where does it all begin?

It is my belief LEOs are born with a genetic disorder called the law enforcement syndrome. Seriously, if you talk with quite a few LEOs, you quickly learn they wanted to go into law enforcement since they were just tiny tots. Quite a few of them will admit to playing "good guy versus bad guy" or "cops and robbers" since they were just itty bitty. My LEO even admits to seeking out bad guys day after day when he was just a small tike, riding his bicycle all over his backyard, pretending to shoot out evil with his black plastic revolvers strapped to his hip, often thinking he was the *only sheriff* in town. When I calculated, I figured he could have only been eight or nine years old. Thus is the proof of the law enforcement syndrome.

Just a technical note here, once they are born with the syndrome, it is not curable. As these tiny tots grow into adults, the syndrome seems to become stronger and perhaps more definitive. As the LEO becomes a young adult, the syndrome seems to reach a peak of seeking out the profession of becoming a cop or deputy. Along with this desire, the "big heart" condition may become apparent. The future LEO may express thoughts of helping others, of saving lives, or fighting crime at all cost.

The ultimate diagnosis becomes apparent when the future LEO seeks out a law enforcement agency which LEO hopes will send them to a law enforcement academy. Once the law enforcement agency sponsors the LEO cadet for an academy, the future LEO will express gratitude and happiness at having the chance to fulfill an ambitious goal of becoming a certified law enforcement officer.

Because of the law enforcement syndrome, the person is willing to go through vigorous steps just to reach the point of being selected for an academy. The future LEO will train to pass physical exertion tests, they will have good ethics and qualities to pass a background check, they will be willing to be wired extensively for a polygraph test, they will be questioned extensively by a psychologist, and they will be subjected to written and oral boards before even being considered for an academy. Yet because of their special makeup, the future LEO looks forward to these challenges to be one step closer to their ultimate dream.

Therefore, if you live with a future LEO, these challenges may not seem as beneficial in your mind as they do in LEO's mind. You are living with person who is living with an uncontrollable condition called the law enforcement syndrome. While the future LEO is euphoric with possibilities, the reality of the profession starts to weigh upon your reality check. Where do I fit in this dream? How do I cope with the preacademy tests?

The future LEO will not show stress or any lack of confidence while taking the preacademy tests due to his/her condition. You, on the other hand, because you do not suffer from law enforcement syndrome may feel overwhelmed with nervous twitches, anxiety, and bouts of relief when he or she passes each test, one by one. Thus, when the testing process is over, you have sweated any small minute excess of body fluid, you have acquired several premature wrinkles, and you seriously have twitched until you have muscle stiffness. You feel years older and somewhat ill for going through the processes. Yet when you look at your future LEO, he or she does not seem any worse for the wear. He/she is triumphant they passed and assure you they knew they did their very best.

About the time you have gathered your wits about you, enough to think you may trudge on within reasonable boundaries of sanity, the law enforcement academy begins. You think to yourself, "How difficult can this be? Thousands of officers and their families have survived the academy and seem to have handled it well. Therefore, we will too." Maybe.

LIVING WITH A LAW ENFORCEMENT ACADEMY CADET

S hine, shine, shine those black boots. Spit on them, rub them until it appears you will rub the black leather off; but shine, shine, shine those boots. In my opinion, academy instructors have an infatuation with shiny black boots. The shinier, the blacker, the better. They also have an infatuation with crisp, ironed uniforms and nice clean-shaven faces.

Law enforcement academy instructors also appear to have supernatural powers they pass down to their cadets; powers that give the cadet calmness in stressful situations, the strength and knowledge to face life-threatening scenarios, techniques to drive like a maniac when called to do so, as well as the comprehension of the laws of the land and how and when to enforce them.

During academy life, the LEO transforms from the quaint civilian into the strong, determined, and neat, very neat, LEO. The transformation is only completed because of dedication and very intensive training on the part of the future LEO. It is during this time the true LEOs find out if they can endure the tests of academy life and tests they may face in their law enforcement careers later.

And how do you endure the academy? When your future LEO is at home and not at the academy, there is really not a significant change in his/her thought process. The reason for this is the whole weekend he/she is still focusing on the academy. The LEO's body is home; the mind is studying laws, thinking over how he or she can improve in defensive tactics, or shining boots. During academy time, your cadet may become noticeably focused on the neatness of his/her attire, your attire, his/her mother's attire, the neighbor's attire. A conversation may go like this:

LEO may say, "Did you ever notice how wrinkled Mr. Groceryman's pants are? The guy apparently never irons them."

You may reply, "No, I have never noticed that before," as you wear the shiniest black shoes you have ever worn because your LEO cadet wanted you to feel special so he polished your black shoes too.

And so begins some of the unpredictable yet sometimes predictable habits of a LEO.

This same obsession becomes focused on his/her duty weapon. A LEO will spend *forever* cleaning his/her gun, polishing it over and over again. Running little cloths and rods through the cylinder over and over. Checking his/her ammo several times. Loading and unloading. The academy stresses the importance of the upkeep of duty weapons as well as the skills to use them. If you are unfamiliar with duty weapons, you will gain in your vocabulary. You will hear words like *caliber*, *ammo*, and *targets* repeated over and over. As long as your LEO is active in duty, these words will always be part of LEO's conversational terminology.

You may hear your LEO tell you, "Once the academy is over, life will be normal." He or she may say it with such conviction, you find yourself with a tendency of wanting to believe them. Honey, honey, honey. Life with a LEO will be anything but normal.

A milestone in life is the graduation day from the law enforcement academy. This day is a day of the past yet a day of the future. From this day forward, your LEO will not be the same as in the past. He or she will become a sworn officer to uphold all laws of the land and the Constitution of the United States and to provide the means to protect them. The dream of that tiny tot playing cops and robbers is of the past, and the goal is now reality. The future is undefined yet exciting as the new LEO faces the heavy responsibilities of serving and protecting the civilian population and his/her brothers and sisters in blue.

For you, this day is a day of infamy. You no longer live with a civilian. You live with a LEO. Excitement surges in your blood as you are handed the badge, which most academies ceremoniously give to the wife, husband, or significant other to pin on the chest of the newly sworn officer. Emotions of happiness swell in your heart yet caution sweeps through you as you realize the challenges and hardships you may face in the future. You shake, hopefully unnoticed, as you stick the pin through the neatly pressed uniform over LEO's heart until you realize you have stuck it too far and your

LEO is trying to hide pain. Sorry. You then cautiously concentrate on placing the badge or star over the heart of the LEO you love. This day is also a day of infamy because you too have made sacrifices and strides; and thus, the moment feels right. A moment when he looks in your eyes and you look in his; time stops and all that surrounds you is insignificant except for him. It is your honor to pin the badge because in many ways, it is your badge too.

And so begins a journey into a trail of a career with ups and downs, mountains and valleys, and tears and laughter. As long as you have a good sense of humor, your LEO will be able to provide you many laughs but not without sacrifices, tears, and an occasional emotional meltdown.

ROOKIE, ROOKIE LEO

S igh of relief. The long (seeming to last a lifetime)
law enforcement academy is over and it is time to
settle back, relax, and get into a halfway decent schedule
of living. When you first start your career as a LEO
supporter, you may find the halfway decent schedule of
living consists of you being home *alone* and your rookie
being at work, working, or working over. Why?

Why? The rookie LEO gains a momentous amount
of knowledge in the academy; but out on the street,
working for a specific law enforcement agency, requires
additional training and instruction. The LEO rookie
will usually be accompanied by a FTO or field training
officer for quite a few weeks, teaching them the necessary
skills the department wants them to acquire. And while
most departments work in similar fashion, there are
variations depending on the individual department.
Also, some law enforcement agencies require the rookie
to complete a post academy specific for their agency.
And is all this training necessary? Absolutely. The
surplus knowledge and training acquired by the rookie
helps enable his or her safety as well as the safety of
the public.

But where is your training? Do you have a field training officer teaching you how to cope with being a LEO supporter? Perhaps sharing safety tips on how to survive on your own, even though you live with a LEO? No. And this is what makes you so special. You have the abilities to blindly step on the edge of life, blindly feeling your way as you go, while not allowing yourself to fall off the edge. You are able to cope with the uphill, the downhill, and the curvy, winding path leading into oblivion.

Does Rookie LEO understand the darkness you face? Absolutely not. Rookie LEO is too busy trying to survive all the new responsibilities and demands of the new profession. The difference? Rookie LEO loves every challenge; Rookie LEO is living in seventh heaven. You, on the other hand, may be struggling with all the demands you did not ask for, such as running the household, paying bills in a timely manner, training the dog, playing with the kids, taking out the trash, vehicle maintenance, and you may feel like you are living in an errand hell (all alone) surrounded by voices squealing, "This needs to be done. This needs to be done. This needs to be done." You may reach a breaking point where you imagine the squealing voices have little LEO faces.

Why all the chaos? The biggest challenge sometimes is the swing shift or night shift your LEO is assigned, along with working what normal people call "weekends."

Rookie LEOs love working weekends in the wee hours of the night. The creatures of crime seem to crawl out of the cracks of the sidewalks and roam the streets just enticing your new LEO to catch them in their wake of criminal behavior. Thus, the law enforcement syndrome may become overly active at this time in LEO's career.

"Damn, I love working nights. Damn, I love working weekends. Damn, the lights look brighter when you are running code. The sirens sound louder. There is more action. A lot more action. More excitement. More arrests. Damn, I love working nights." These may be the words your rookie LEO appears to have been programmed to repeat over and over. You may ask yourself repeatedly, "Where is LEO's switch so I can shut him or her *off*? Damn, I can't find it. Damn, I am tired of hearing about lights and sirens. Damn, I can't find that *turn off* switch."

Because the law enforcement syndrome is acquired at birth or earlier, the turn off switch is not available in the LEO model of human kind. As long as they breathe, they will breathe law enforcement.

SPEAK THE LINGO

B y now, you have been exposed to the new language of police or law enforcement codes. You have probably heard police calls being dispatched over the radio in a manner such as this:

"P505," the dispatcher will say.

"P505," the officer will respond.

"Please 10-19 to the east-bound side of Highway 8, milepost 210. We have a report of a male subject on foot weaving in and out of traffic. The subject is wearing a light blue shirt, blue jeans, and a dark ball cap," the dispatcher will instruct.

"10-4, en route to Highway 8," the officer will declare.

The outcome of this situation can be questionable. For example, if the officer is very close to mile post 210, you may hear the following:

"P505," the officer.

"P505," the dispatcher.

"I'm 10-97. I will be out with Dodger Lucky. First name of David, Ocean, David, George, Edward, Robert. Last name with spelling Lincoln, Union, Charles, King, Young. Date of birth 10/19/86."

After the dispatcher runs the individual in the criminal computer system, you may hear the officer say, "Code 4. I'll be 10-15, to the county."

The interpretation is the officer received a call of a male running in and out of traffic, arrived on scene, arrested the individual, and continued to transport the male subject to the county incarceration facility.

The very same dispatch call could have an altogether different outcome with the officer declaring, "I'm 10-97. We have a male subject down with minor injuries. Subject's name is Dodger Unlucky. First name spelling David, Ocean, David, George, Edward, Robert. Last name spelling Union, Nancy, Lincoln, Union, Charles, King, Young. Date of birth 10/19/86. Please send medical."

The interpretation for this outcome is the male subject probably wasn't quite as fast as necessary to dodge the oncoming vehicles and got clipped by one, injuring the male subject slightly.

And then there is a more finale outcome. The officer may declare, "I'm 10-97. We have a male subject down. Subject's name is Dodger Nomore. First name spelling David, Ocean, David, George, Edward, Robert. Last name spelling Nancy, Ocean, Mary, Ocean, Robert, Edward. Date of birth 10/19/86. Please send medical. 10-22 running code 3."

This means poor Dodger Nomore is DRT or dead right there and will not be able to dodge vehicles except in the afterlife.

The example shows how your LEO can never predict the ending of a call or the call itself. A simple call can turn into a very complicated and sometimes disturbing situation. Therefore, the code system was inducted into law enforcement as a safety precaution so not everyone, especially criminals, will know exactly what is going on but dispatch and the officer will. The alphabet code came into place so the dispatcher could readily understand the spelling of names or the alphabet letters of vehicle tags.

Do you need a code manual? If you listen to a police scanner when your LEO is working, you may want to learn the codes. At first, the language may seem complicated, but before you know it, you will be speaking to LEO in their own terms.

"P505," you will say.

"P505," the officer will respond.

"10-19 to your 10-42. I have Code 7 available," you will instruct which means, "Come home to your house. I have supper ready."

Hopefully, if the officer isn't too busy, he or she will respond, "10-4," which means "okay."

ACCEPT THE MISTRESS

(Apology to female LEOs and their supporters. This chapter is written in the male version. Please substitute the word mistress *with* man candy, *he* for *she, etc., to correct for gender.)*

She is charming, captivating, and very, very enticing. She sees your handsome LEO, dressed ever so attractive in his uniform of black, gun at his hip, and badge on his heart; and she declares prey. She is intrigued by his gallant presence, his stature of confidence, and his heroic chivalry. She wants him. She wants him *bad.* She lures him into her clutches, she takes him into the dangers of the night, and she tantalizes him with her seductive attributes. He is weak when it comes to her. He cannot say "*no.*"

She is Law Enforcement. Law Enforcement cares not that he is married or "hooked up" with someone. She demands all of him. Law Enforcement demands all of his mental attention. She demands all of him physically; she demands all of him emotionally. And what does she give him in return?

Law Enforcement has attributes the LEO supporter cannot compete with. First of all, she is a mistress of the heart, not a physical being. Second, she has her own language, her own way of communication to keep him close to her. This mistress tantalizes with an adrenaline rush when a threatening call on society is at hand; she gives him a euphoric high when he handles the call safely and successfully. She has high-class toys such as sirens; strobing, flashing blue lights; Taser guns; and more. She is relentless in her call to him, and unless you, as a LEO supporter, have extraordinary gadgets and powers in your possession, you are more than likely going to experience the tug of his mistress, Law Enforcement.

Even when LEOs tire of the long, long hours, the emotional crash after a hot call, they cannot leave her for very long. Curiosity about their mistress gets the best of them. LEOs may listen to the scanner when not on duty to find out what she is up to. They may even check in at the station to see where she is as far as calls go. And you will find your LEO possessive of Law Enforcement, to the point you may hear something like this:

"They had a homicidal suspect barricaded at the market early this morning. The suspect apparently was shooting the place up with a .9mm (gun). Spraying bullets all over. Man, I wish they had called me. I would have contemplated setting up the perimeter and looked at making entry on the south side of the building, yada, yada, yada."

And you? You try to appear sympathetic by saying something like, "Honey, I'm so, so, so sorry they did not think to call you. I'm sure they would have called you immediately if you had not worked the last forty-eight hours straight, day and night, until your eyes are all glassy, swollen, and you look like hell. Honey, don't worry. I'm sure you will be the first they call next time."

The most difficult task at hand is realizing Law Enforcement is his mistress and not some hussy of flesh and bones. This may be harder than you think. It is not at all uncommon to be in public, and some young cute thing run up to your LEO exclaiming she was so glad he came to her rescue in the bar last night.

It is also a normal human trait to be jealous of your LEO. For example, you may accuse him or her of having an affair or affairs (plural) because of the amount of time they dedicate to their profession away from you. You may have a conversation like the following:

"Just be honest with me. Are you having an affair? You spend so many hours away from home. What am I suppose to think? Who was that little blond slutty-looking girl who said you did such a good job with her friend last night? Who is her friend? Are you in love with her friend? How do you know her friend? Do you love her friend?" you heatedly ask.

"No, I don't love her friend, but apparently, her friend loves me, and it must have been love at first sight because last night when I was on duty, I got a call to go to a disturbance at the Beyond Intoxicated Bar on the west side of town. The minute I showed up to arrest her friend, her friend kept yelling, 'Fuck you. Fuck you.'"

And to drive the point home, your LEO may chuckle and say, "Yeah, I'm pretty sure it was love at first sight because she was still yelling 'Fuck you' when

I booked her into jail, only her words were slurred like, 'Fuuuuckkkk whyuuuuuuu.'"

Do you feel a little guilty for falsely accusing LEO? Not really. It doesn't hurt to get these matters settled. Hopefully, you will feel better, and the officer will feel better because now you know the little blond slutty-looking girl's friend is locked away. At least it was just Law Enforcement he was with and not someone of flesh and blood.

IT IS OKAY TO BE JEALOUS

"How's LEO? What did they have going last night?"

"How's LEO? I saw LEO directing traffic when they had that big collision on Crash Street. How did that all turn out?"

"How's LEO? I think LEO was running with lights and siren south to Meth-ville yesterday. Did they have something go down?"

"How's LEO? Did they ever catch that armed robber that robbed Cash Mart?"

"How's LEO? How's LEO? How's LEO?" It sometimes appears everyone wants to know how's LEO. What about, "How's LEO's supporter?" On very few occasions will someone actually inquire about you.

"How's LEO's supporter? I saw them shopping yesterday with groceries piled sky high and the kids hanging recklessly off the side of the basket."

Or "How's LEO's supporter? I saw them out chopping weeds in the Yard of Jungle Doom?"

Or "How's LEO's supporter? Were they pulling their hair out in little ringlets while they foamed incoherently at the mouth because they live with LEO?"

Most friends and family will inquire about LEO first and, maybe by the end of the conversation, ask about you. By then, the conversation has gone on so long that you may just answer you are okay and leave it at that. Or unfortunately sometimes when you start to ramble about some of your projects, the listener may cut you off prematurely, exclaiming it is time for them to go. Alrighty, then.

Is it normal to be jealous of LEO and the profession? I believe it is normal, and one should not feel guilty about being jealous.

For example, you may ask your LEO what they did today. It may go as follows:

"I tracked a rape suspect on Perpetrator Row until I found footprints leading into the forest. I called for backup but pursued this individual on foot, running as fast as I could. I caught up with him, tackled him, wrestled with him until he was in handcuffs and placed into the cage of my patrol car, all before my backup arrived. I booked him into jail and then proceeded to take a call of a speeding vehicle. I located the said vehicle parked north of the junction and found three older individuals very intoxicated of which I arrested the driver DUI and transported to jail. I also towed the vehicle because none of the passengers were capable of driving in their condition. I then proceeded to run code (with lights and siren) to a domestic in progress. I detained and arrested the female subject and had the male subject transported to the hospital for injuries sustained with a ball bat. What did you do today?"

"*Wow.* Well, I took the kids to the grocery store. I pulled weeds in the lawn. I tried a new toilet bowl cleaner which really makes the bowl look so, so shiny. Do you want to see?"

So while it is very difficult to overcome the jealousy of the excitement LEO sees on a daily basis, you should realize it is you, the strong corner block of the foundation that renders the stability of the household for your family and LEO as well. And while cleaning the toilet bowl isn't as exciting as catching perpetrators, it is just as necessary.

You are probably asking yourself, "Will LEO ever have time to clean the toilet?"

Maybe someday, but it will never be as clean as when you do it.

THE SUSPICION ALERT

B y the time your rookie LEO has traveled passed the initial learning phase of law enforcement, it may become evident your LEO possesses a distinct personality disorder from being born with the law enforcement syndrome. Perhaps, the best term for this disorder is *suspicious*.

While suspicious is a trait that will inevitably serve them well in the law enforcement profession (perhaps even save their life), it can sometimes be a little trying to live with the "suspicious" LEO.

For example, your family is on vacation (probably a very long overdue one). Perhaps, you have been lucky enough to go to an amusement park with your children. Everyone around you is laughing and giggling and running with enthusiasm to the next ride or amusement. That is everyone, but LEO. You turn to see what LEO is doing because LEO has been so quiet. Slowly, LEO is making their way through the crowd of young children and adults, watching everyone intently, looking at Ms. Gothic Teen who is sporting multiple body piercings as if the young girl were armed and dangerous. There is no smile on LEO's face; there is a stern, "I'm scoping this place out" look.

You may yell back at LEO, "Honey, are you having a good time?"

"Oh, yes," LEO replies as he or she double-checks (unnoticeably to civilians) to see if their off-duty weapon is accessible.

Part of LEO's training and instruction focuses on the ability to recognize something unusual and to question the reason for it. At work, this is absolutely necessary. But at home, it can sometimes be a little bizarre. For example, the pastor of the church stops by your house to leave some pamphlets. He seems like a nice enough guy; but for some reason, your LEO feels there is something suspicious about him. He just doesn't "add up." After he pulls out of the driveway, your LEO runs fast outside to inspect your vehicles thoroughly to be sure Pastor Shady didn't damage any on his way out.

And to your surprise, your LEO comments convincingly, "Yeah, he's the type to hit them and never admit it." Wow.

While you think he is being overly critical and *suspicious*, you have learned to trust his instincts because more than likely LEO may be right. After the visit, you cannot look at Pastor Shady the same way because you just know it was him that left that little white mark on your front bumper.

If LEO can be this mistrusting of a pastor, heaven only help the criminals.

And haven't we all heard LEO ask, "Who stopped by the house today? There are fresh tire tracks in the drive."

Perhaps, it is times like these you realize not everyone's mate notices fresh tire tracks or any tire tracks for that matter. Other mates are probably looking at the beautiful red roses in bloom or enjoying the beautiful multicolored rainbow in the beautiful blue sky. But not your LEO; your LEO is scoping out the tire tracks, and that is what makes your LEO so special.

In your heart, you know LEO could never be a LEO supporter married to a LEO identical to himself or herself. It would drive them absolutely crazy with suspicious thoughts. There's no way they could cope with their LEO telling them, "I'm working a homicide case, taking longer than I thought, try to be home by first light, yada, yada, yada…" or "I'm going to be working over, trying to catch the burglar by Boobsy Bar, don't know when I will see you." To be honest, they are not patient enough or trusting enough to live with their identical LEO, and that's what makes you so special.

DO YOU KNOW WHO YOU ARE?

S afety, by now, has probably become a focus in your household: How to keep LEO safe, how to keep yourself safe, how to keep your kids safe.

Sometimes, the best safety plan is evaluate, evaluate, evaluate and go from there. For instance, many people in passing may catch your last name and ask if you are related to the law enforcement officer with the same last name. For mainstream society, it is not a problem usually to reveal their relationship to others and their identity. However, because of the criminal element our LEOs deal with, sometimes on a very regular basis, it is usually best to avoid identifying your relationship with LEO if you suspect a person may use it in a derogatory way against you or your LEO.

Therefore, if Burly Bar'brawler hears your last name and automatically questions in a loud and demanding way, "Are you kin to that son of a bitch who arrested me and threw my ass in jail for five days?" You know to exclaim, "Why no, I didn't even know there was an officer with the same last name as me."

If a nice elderly lady who is an elementary teacher says your LEO is the most gallant and sweetest officer she has ever met and asks if you are related, more than likely it is going to be okay to tell her very proudly that yes you are related.

But what about the ones that fall in between? Those that seem a little on the good side and a little on the bad side? Some techniques which have worked successfully for me is to talk very fast about how much I like their head full of dreads and inquire how to maintain them, or I quickly ask them if they are related to the elderly gentleman standing three feet away "because there is such a striking resemblance," even if he is of a different ethnicity than they are. One may be able to think of many clever ways to avoid answering the relationship question.

A cautionary note: if you wait too long to acknowledge the question by a pregnant silence as you try to evaluate what to say, the person asking may start talking to you in a very loud, distinct voice implying you are confused, and ask, "Hey, lady, are you all right? Do you know who you are?" Then, you may become worried they will call the police due to a very confused female who apparently does not know who she is.

Children are smart, spontaneous little beings who seem not to struggle with the identity question. You may hear your children answer in reference to their father, "Oh, he is a distant cousin to my great-great-uncle," or "I've never heard of him," or "He's the odd sheep of the family tree. We never talk to him." Clever,

clever those young ones. Hopefully, for LEO's sake they won't say he is their "great-great-great-great-grandpa."

None of us like to lie or tell untruths, but occasionally because you and your children live with a LEO, it may become necessary to keep all safe.

TIPS FOR SURVIVING
LIFE WITH LEO

Just as some occasions warrant being careful acknowledging your identity, there are also situations it is just better for all to be silent. Silent about what?

When you live with LEO, there are certain situations you will encounter. For instance, a very prominent citizen in the community, Mr. Monetary, has been arrested on theft charges because he seemingly needs to supply money for his gambling problem. The way you know this is you overheard your LEO talking on the phone with a supervising LEO. Should you

A. Call the newspaper right away because this is juicy gossip the whole town should know?

B. Call your friend, Mary TalkToAnyOne, so she will know the scoop?

C. Answer in minute detail everything you know about the case only if asked by relatives and close friends?

D. Remain silent and appear ignorant of the case no matter who asks questions?

Let's explore the options. If you chose A, more than likely you misheard the details and Mr. Monetary will personally sue you and LEO for everything you have ever hoped to own. Also, LEO will get fired, but the Fiction Tab Newspaper will love you for your contribution because newspaper sales went through the roof. If you chose B or C, by the time Mary TalkToAnyOne has circulated part truth and part drama in regards to Mr. Monetary, Mr. Monetary will sue you and LEO and your circle of friends and family for defamation of character because it was circulated he needed money to pay for his sex addiction. Also, LEO will get fired. The correct answer is D. You should *absolutely not* divulge any information *whatsoever*. If you supply details of this case to anyone *at all*, you have jeopardized LEO's job and the case of the theft. What goes on with LEO's work must stay with LEO. Appearing dumb is better than your LEO being unemployed and angry with you because you could not be quiet, and LEO griping about living out on the streets with the homeless because you are being sued by Mr. Monetary for eternity.

Another survival tip is to be very observant of your surroundings and home. I suggest if Johnny MethHead follows you from the grocery store to your driveway, you should

A. *Not* turn in. Drive down the street, slowly feel for your loaded .357 revolver, make a call to

LEO to let them know what is happening, and drive back to a law enforcement agency parking lot as safely and as quickly as possible.

B. Pull into your driveway, stand gun ready behind your vehicle door, and start firing your loaded .357 at Johnny's car until there are no more bullets left.

C. Pull into Mrs. NoseyNeighbor's drive because you don't like her anyway.

D. Pull into your drive, run hard to let your "I will eat the rubber off your tires" guard dog loose, and watch with amusement as Johnny MethHead mangles with "Killer."

Of course, the correct answer is A. If you chose B, LEO's friends will be forced to work overtime, especially if you hit Johnny MethHead with a bullet, injuring him or worse. If you chose C, Mrs. NoseyNeighbor will never, ever let you live it down, and you will live in neighborhood hell *forever*. And if you chose D, while it might be very entertaining "Killer," the guard dog, playing with Johnny, there could be lots of blood which you will inevitably have to clean up. On top of that, you will have to explain your actions to LEO. Yes, A is definitely the correct answer.

Personally, I feel more secure having a gun on board. I have completed a Carry Concealed Weapons (CCW) course, and I am glad I did. I pray I will never have to use my .357, but if I need to in order to protect my family or myself, I feel confident I will be able to do so.

When children are small, a "don't touch, hands off, keep the guns locked up" approach to handling firearms is best until children are old enough to understand the dangers associated with guns; gun *safety* is an *absolute*. In a LEO's house, educating your children early and continually, over and over, about gun safety and gun danger is a requirement because of the exposure they receive on a daily basis. As the child matures, you may opt to place them in a gun safety class as well.

Next scenario: your LEO has been working swing shift and you feel restless after your children go to bed. You should

A. Go to the bars in hopes of seeing your LEO and get acquainted with the people he/she arrests on a regular basis (or what LEO may refer to as his/her "frequent fliers" or "repeat clientele").

B. Watch a scary, scary movie so you think the Boogey Man is in your house and you are terrified.

C. Pace up and down the hallway until your legs give out or LEO comes home.

D. Find a hobby you enjoy and treasure your accomplishments.

While other choices are options, I believe the most satisfying one for a long-term relationship with LEO is choice D.

In the world of Facebook, Twitter, and various other Internet connections, you may want to be cautious of the information you supply online, such as going on vacation or when LEO is at an out-of-town training. Due to the unethical thinking of the criminal mind, it merits taking precautions to be safe. However, if you want to share "Killer" being "friendly" with Johnny MethHead, that is entirely up to you.

LEO'S SMALL KIDS:
ARE THEY INFLUENCED
BY LAW ENFORCEMENT?

Does law enforcement affect LEO's children? As hard as you try to live like a "normal" family, there are times it is evident law enforcement does have an effect on your children.

When small tikes are just starting school, they may very rarely see LEO if LEO leaves for work just before they are returning home from school and LEO is sleeping when they are leaving for school in the mornings. Because time passes so slowly when we are very young, to the young child, it may seem like an eternity since they have seen LEO. The small tike may inquire, "Does Daddy (or Mama) still live here?"

Also, depending on the caseload, your LEO may be spending extra time on duty, or working an extensive case. If the family dog, "Killer," becomes very agitated, barking and quite defensive, when he hears the police unit drive up, it may be necessary to reacquaint your pets and children with your LEO.

"Killer, down boy, down boy. Quit biting his leg. It's LEO, you crazy dog." You may even need to continue: "And, LEO, this is your daughter, Little Sprout, and your son, Small Tot. Kids, do you remember LEO?"

Children soak information up like a sponge when intrigued. Therefore, if there is an altercation on the playground, and Ms. Kindergarten Teacher is trying to decipher which little boy is telling the truth, it may not be uncommon for your offspring to step in and ask each one, "Do you swear to tell the truth, the whole truth, and may God so help you?"

Isn't that just cute? Instead of "so help you God," Small Tot has interpreted it as "may God so help you."

LEO's children may grow up thinking it is perfectly normal to hear terminology like brass, holster, Glock, .9mm, handcuffs, ammo, Taser, etc. Also, LEO's children learn the rules of gun safety at a very, very early age. Because of this important "hands off" training, LEOs will hide and secure guns but will often leave ammo scattered *everywhere*. Little Sprout and Small Tot may not think it unusual to find bullets in the candy dish because LEO thinks it's handy or ammo in the floorboard of the old family truck because LEO wants to go target shooting.

It is important to note most LEOs are absolutely "anal" about the placement of their guns when they are off duty to be sure the guns are locked and secure away from little hands. However, LEOs tend to leave bullets and bullet magazines lying all over in what they describe as "easy places to get to them"—thus, candy dishes, floorboards of old trucks, the living room coffee table, on top of the refrigerator, in the nightstand, in the bathroom medicine cabinet, the television cabinet, etc. And while Little Sprout and Small Tot grow accustom to this trait, visitors to your house may still show a surprised, questioning look when they spot the pile of ammo in the rare antique vase Aunt Saveitall gave you.

You may find yourself defending LEO's habit by inquiring, "Doesn't everyone put ammo in their antique vases?"

Little Sprout may even exclaim, "When I grow up, I'm going to be a LEO. And I want to have enough money to fill every dish with bullets."

This is normal. Isn't it?

DO LEO'S SMALL KIDS INFLUENCE THEM?

The sense of humor you have acquired over time from living with LEO has somehow passed on to your little ones. Little Sprout and Small Tot have no problem enjoying a good sense of humor, sometimes at LEO's expense.

For example, if your LEO comes home in a lethargic state after working a tremendously stressful situation, he or she may sit in a quiet trance seeming to watch television while actually traveling into a world of "I'm too tired and exhausted to care." It is in this state that your LEO is most vulnerable at home, and your children know it. Little Sprout may take this opportunity to place bright pink earrings on his ears and place necklaces around his neck, playing "dress up." How does LEO react? He is simply too tired and exhausted to care. LEO's given name is Don. Little Sprout renames him "Donnella" for the sake of playing dress up with him.

You chuckle. You laugh. You even deny the overwhelming urge to take a picture of him. All is well until Little Sprout comes home the next day from school, so proud of the fact she shared at "Show and Tell." When you ask her what she shared, she informs you, "I told everyone Daddy likes to play dress up like a girl with pink earrings and necklaces, and we call him Donnella."

Okay, then. How to approach LEO with this news? While you chuckled and laughed last night, somehow, you know LEO is not going to find this as humorous as you do.

Small Tot has recently become fascinated with LEO's handcuffs. While LEO is home on lunch break from being a field training officer (FTO), Small Tot asks if he can play with LEO's handcuffs. LEO lets him. Small Tot asks if he can place the handcuffs on LEO. LEO sees no harm in this and lets him. Small Tot asks if he can unlock the handcuffs he has placed on LEO. LEO sees no harm in this and lets him try to unlock the handcuffs. Small Tot breaks the key off in the handcuffs. *What? Small Tot breaks the key?* It is the only handcuff key in the house.

There LEO stands dressed in full uniform with hands handcuffed behind, sporting a demanding presence with a stern face. Somehow, the handcuffs are going to have to be removed, but how? Too embarrassing to call for a fellow officer to bring a key. LEO would never, ever live that down.

This job calls for a hacksaw to grind through the metal and someone not laughing hysterically to do the job. You cannot help yourself. You are laughing so hard tears are streaming down your face as you hold the phone to LEO's ear so LEO can call the cadet in training and tell them he has been "detained" at lunch a little longer than he thought he would be. "Detained?" How funny is that?

You wipe the tears of laughter away enough to try to move the hacksaw back and forth, sawing through the metal carefully without sawing the bare skin. You are not oblivious to the fact Little Sprout and Small Tot are giggling uncontrollably as they run circles around and around LEO during this process, shouting, "We arrested you. We arrested you. You are caught. You are caught."

The unforgettable stress in LEO's face sends an apparent message this little episode will remain a top secret. All LEO needs is for the training cadet to get word of how his/her FTO was handcuffed by Small Tot and was "detained."

Sometimes, it is through the mouths of babes we find who we are or what our limitations are. LEO children seem to be very talented at seeing the world with clarity when it comes to inspecting the strengths and weaknesses of LEO.

For example, there is a vicious dog at large in the neighborhood. LEO has been called upon to tranquilize the uncontrollable canine. A big Saturday morning crowd has gathered about the dog, cautiously standing outside of the gated, fenced premise where the dog growls, foaming and barking ferociously. As it happens, Small Tot is with LEO but has been placed in a vehicle at quite some distance from the dog for Small Tot's safety.

LEO bravely approaches to the cheers of the multiple onlookers. LEO loads the tranquilizer gun as the crowd proudly looks on, glad LEO is there to protect them and their neighborhood. LEO takes in a breath of pride, proud that he is able to save the day (actually like a knight in shining armor). Destroyer Dog is now chewing the corner trim from the stranger's house, biting away one chump at a time, growling with evil, evil warning. LEO is thankful it is the house being chewed and not a person.

LEO evaluates the crowd, lifts the tranquilizer gun, pauses so the crowd can witness LEO's valor and gallantry, takes aim at the vicious canine, dramatically pulls the trigger for the benefit of the spectators, and completely misses the dog with the syringe hitting against the house and falling to the ground, provoking the dog even more.

What? Misses?

LEO can't believe it. Missing a shot. To add to LEO's embarrassment, the little voice of Small Tot yells from the vehicle, "Hey, Dad, you a little rusty?" to which the crowd roars with laughter.

So much for gallantry.

MYTHS AND TRUTHS ABOUT LAW ENFORCEMENT OFFICERS

Are law enforcement officers taught "The Officer Stance"?

You probably have witnessed several times how when a group of LEOs come together, even off duty, they all stand in a line, feet shoulder length apart, arms crossed in front, standing at a "casual" attention, conversing by turning their necks either to the right or left. The group of LEOs may find humor in the conversation and will laugh hysterically without moving from "The Stance." Why is this?

It is my belief this could be a carry over genetic position they suffer from their law enforcement syndrome. "The Stance" seems to be indicative of their profession to the point if you take LEO camping for weeks, and LEO grows a wild mess of whiskers and smells intolerable, the public still will be able to tell he is a law enforcement officer because of "The Stance." You may hear someone ask the bearded, dark nasty LEO, "You're a cop, aren't you?" So the old saying, you can take LEO away from law enforcement, but you can't take law enforcement from LEO is absolutely true.

Is it a requirement for male LEOs to shave their heads bald like Bruce Willis after they lose some on top?

Each law enforcement agency varies as to regulations concerning body hair. However, there does seem to be a trend of shiny bald heads among the male LEO community. Once again, it is my belief this could be a direct notion associated with the law enforcement syndrome.

LEOs seem to be driven by distinct lines and rules. For example, the suspect is either guilty or not guilty (no in between such as the suspect is a little guilty). The person in question has either been drinking or not drinking (no in between such as only drinking a sip or two). The repeat perpetrator needs to be incarcerated for life (not incarcerated until the jail is too full or he/she has displayed good enough behavior in prison to be paroled). LEOs distinguish lines and boundaries. I believe it is this trait that influences them to shave their heads. You are either totally bald or have hair (not just a few tufts here and there).

Do LEOs know what time it is?

If LEO is waiting on you for a dinner date, LEO absolutely knows the correct time and how many minutes and seconds you are late. LEOs, bless their hearts, have been burdened with becoming agitated if they have to wait on someone for anything, criminal or not.

However, LEOs have also been burdened with what I refer to as "law enforcement time confusion disorder," which refers to confusion of the correct time when they are working a law enforcement case. It is not uncommon for LEO to be expected in ten minutes and arrive an hour and ten minutes later due to a call or case. In an extreme condition of this disorder, the LEO may even arrive three hours and ten minutes behind schedule exclaiming, "I didn't know it was getting so late."

Unfortunately, this disorder when provoked can progress into an extreme "ignore" condition. No matter how many texts, phone calls, and voice mails you send to LEO, you may be placed on "ignore" if the law enforcement call LEO is working is life threatening. Hopefully, when the call is completed, LEO will also possess the gift of sweet persuasion so when he/she does arrive home, he/she does not face a life-threatening situation twice in one day.

Do LEOs have similar thinking patterns as mainstream society?

As stated earlier, they do seem to waiver from the norm when in large crowds, etc., due to their defensive training. However, I believe LEOs are very capable of similar thinking patterns, but I also believe similar thinking patterns are not normal for them. For instance, your LEO comes home on what you consider an ordinary day. Upon arrival, your LEO exclaims in a very matter of fact way that LEO wants to start building a new house, buy a new car, and have a baby.

Wow. What happened in LEO's day to stimulate thinking of all these life-changing events? You thought of buying a new rug for the front door but not building a house, buying a car, and having a baby. *Wow.*

When questioned as to why all of these life-changing events came to mind, LEO replies, "Oh, I was just thinking."

Okay then. Just thinking.

THE ICK FACTOR AND
I SMELL DEAD PEOPLE

If your LEO attends an autopsy, be prepared. LEO will be so excited about witnessing this scientific process of the deceased body that LEO will want to share every little detail with you, thinking you will be as excited over the details as them.

Not. By the time LEO describes some of the procedure, more than likely you may look a little green and feel very queasy as if a good vomit would be a great interruption. The description may go as follows:

"The (autopsy) techs take this saw, and they grind around the top of the head, grr, grr, grr, until they reach this gray liquid matter of what is left of the brain. Grr, grr, grr. And the smell of it all is unbelievable, talk about strong-smelling body decaying odor. Whew. But it doesn't seem to bother the techs one bit. They struggle with prongs or forceps or whatever to pull the brain out, and they are just tugging and tugging and tugging. They remark that poor Decaying Joe must not have been very bright because his brain was littler than most and didn't weigh very much."

"Well, anyway, they saw down the midsection of Decaying Joe and split him right in half on his front skin. Dr. Autopsy advises them to go with caution near the abdomen area. The smell of the putrid body fluids oozing beneath the skin is indescribable. I have never smelled anything as rotten, stronger than rotten eggs I tell you. Dr. Autopsy pulls out the large intestines, tug, tug, tug, examining every inch of poor Joe's inners, and the intestines look grayer than I thought they would, all wrinkled and such with this filmy, milky looking like sticky substance.... decaying, decomposing...black discharging liquid..."

Okay, enough. A good vomit at this point is a very welcomed interruption.

LEOs get excited about the science of the body. They are immune to gore simply because they focus on the investigative side of the criminal investigation of the human carcass. LEOs are able to disassociate Decaying Joe's individuality and persona with the body and simply view the corpse as a tool to lead them to the perpetrator of the crime. We, on the other hand, may stop to reflect if Decaying Joe had children or what his accomplishments in life may have been. We think of Decaying Joe's personality and who he may have been. We think we smell Decaying Joe even though we were never close to the autopsy room.

Puke, puke, puke.

The seasoned officer sees more gore than any of us care to hear about. Automobile accidents can mangle the human body beyond belief, and LEOs are the ones who witness the devastation firsthand. Blood and gore become investigative tools for LEO. Gunshot wounds are a prime example of this. The detective will be able to recreate many crime scenes by blood splatter on walls. And while you like sharing your day with LEO, you may not want them to share all the aspects of their day.

Clorox bleach is truly a lifesaver for LEO. Clorox bleach is LEO's best friend. When exposure to blood through crime scenes or scuffles with bloody suspects, it is not uncommon for LEO to rinse bare skin with pure bleach to minimize the chances of exposure to hepatitis, HIV, and other blood-spore-related diseases. One LEO became exposed to AIDS during a death investigation. He actually took Clorox bleach, full strength, and rinsed his mouth with it. Precautions such as these become part of LEO's professional life. Rubber gloves are also an absolute must in order to protect the officer. Once these exposures occur, the officer is usually required to have blood drawn periodically to insure the exposure has not progressed into indications of the diseases. Therefore, it is not uncommon for huge amounts of Clorox to be used by LEOs.

And you may experience the following: Your LEO is exiting his/her police unit, and you are so, so happy, happy to see LEO. You run full force to give LEO a big hug and tell LEO how blissful you are he/she is home. You want to hug them, you want to kiss them, you want to hug them—*but wait!* LEO is holding both hands up in front, palms facing you in a *stop* motion. "What is it?" you inquire.

"Need the Clorox. Need to wash down," LEO replies.

You stop in your tracks. You don't want to hug LEO if LEO has touched dead people. You do an about-face and run for the Clorox.

You will know LEO's case has turned ugly, ugly if LEO exits his/her patrol car and *you smell dead people*. No words have to be exchanged. You automatically do an about-face and run for the Clorox.

LEO, GROCERY SHOPPING, AND EATING

L EOs are different creatures when it comes to eating and grocery shopping. They may range from caring immensely to not caring at all. The first task at hand is grocery shopping. If your LEO goes with you to the grocery store, a variety of scenarios may take place. First and foremost, LEO may dodge, duck, or play disappearing magic if LEO spots someone he/she does not care to deal with at shopping time.

"Oh crap. There's Margie ComplainAlot. Why is she shopping now?" You may turn and look and LEO has disappeared faster than David Copperfield. Guess LEO didn't want to visit with her.

Then, you may see Hal Repeat'Offender. Your LEO will not be able to focus because LEO thinks there could possibly be an outstanding warrant on ole Hal.

If you get past these setbacks, you may hear LEO complain the whole time you are shopping about how he/she thinks grocery stores should issue citations to customers going down the wrong side of the aisle.

Shoppers should always, always stay on the right side of the aisle to ensure faster usage to others. Perhaps, Grocery *Stop* Citations can be issued to those shoppers who refuse to stop at the end of the aisle before proceeding to their next destination due to putting other shoppers at risk of a basket collision. Think of the revenue grocery stores will "beef up" from citations, no pun intended.

You start looking over the grocery list, the one carefully scrutinized by LEO. LEO likes to make a menu because LEO likes order. Therefore, the grocery list is carefully construed from the menu—not too much of any product, not too little, just enough. Okay.

(Just a precautionary note: LEO may become addicted to organizing your pantry, refrigerator, and freezer by categorizing, alphabetizing, etc. I believe this to be associated with the chaos of law enforcement. While LEO cannot always control things at work, he/she can control the pantry, refrigerator, and freezer. Unless, of course, you have a type B personality also living in the household who really does not mind throwing the opened bag of potato chips on the bottom shelf with alphabetized canned goods instead of the top shelf with the categorized perishable chips and crackers.)

LEO believes one should construe their grocery lists carefully; anything not listed should not be purchased. This serves two functions: one does not make compulsive purchases and one does not buy products to waste. Isn't living with LEO just a *hoot* sometimes? Promptly retrieving the grocery items from the shelf is also important to LEO who believes one should grab the item off the shelf quickly, not pondering or lingering.

LEO may even pridefully remark as you head to the checkout, "Do you realize we beat Margie ComplainAlot and Hal Repeat'Offender by far?"

Funny, I didn't realize we were in competition with them.

Many of you may wonder if your LEO eats or inhales his/her food and other LEOs do not. All LEOs inhale their food. The reasoning is many, many times when LEO is on duty, LEO will just sit down to eat and get a hot, hot call. Early on, LEO learns to gulp food as quickly as possible because this may be the last food he/she gets to ingest for quite a while, depending on the workload.

You may surmise how fast LEO can eat by the way your children react. LEO comes home, Code 7 at 10-42. You watch in amazement as LEO, neatly dressed in uniform, sits scrunched in the dining chair because of the duty holster and gun and gobbles up the meal you have prepared in approximately five minutes. It took you longer to set the table. And to your astonishment, Little Sprout and Small Tot watch with total amusement, placing bets on how fast LEO will be able to down the last bite. You are really in trouble if they start inviting friends over to watch.

How do you handle this? Do you say, "Kids, don't eat as fast as LEO. It's bad for your health"? Or do you look adoringly at LEO and say, "Good job. Way to eat all that's on your plate"?

The irony is after years of eating quickly, LEO is unable to slow down his/her eating habit. You will find you are sitting at the table, eating alone for about fifteen minutes because LEO has already ate, read the paper, cleared his/her side of the table, put food away, and did his/her dishes, and is staring at you while you finish your meal, inquiring, "Why do you eat so *slow*?"

As discussed in a previous chapter, sometimes because of the intensity of law enforcement, LEO may enter a state of "I don't have enough energy to care," or "I have made so many decisions lately, you decide." This state may carry over to food products.

For example, you may ask, "What kind of fish do you want? Do you want baked, fried, or grilled?" LEO may answer, "I don't care, you decide. I'll eat whatever fish you tell me to eat."

You may inquire, "Hamburger is on sale, would you like to cook out on the grill, honey?"

"I don't care, you decide. I will grill out if you tell me to."

You may be at a gourmet ice cream store full of delicious unique flavors of creamy, rich ice cream treats, and you will ask LEO, "Honey, what flavor do you want?"

"I don't care, you decide. I will eat whatever flavor you tell me to."

Funny answer for a LEO who only likes vanilla. "Yes, we will have one vanilla scoop on a plain, drab cone." And LEO is perfectly content licking his/her vanilla cone in a quiet little corner in his/her quiet little way.

LEO'S SENSE OF HUMOR

Just as you have found it necessary to find a sense of humor to survive life with LEO, so too must LEO find a sense of humor to survive his/her law enforcement career. To the average Joe citizen, this sense of humor may appear morbid in nature, but to LEO, it is the gift of survival.

Two deputies respond to a possible suicide. No one has seen Melancholy Doom for six days, and neighbors are beginning to become concerned because the papers are stacking up on the front porch of his house. Melancholy has diligently read the paper early every morning for nearly twenty years. To let the papers stack up is totally out of his character. Dispatch has tried several times to reach him by phone to no avail. It is now time to enter the premises to find out what is wrong.

The deputies clear an empty house; no one in the premises. The big red barn out back needs to be investigated. As the deputies near the entrance, the smell of death permeates the hot summer breeze as the buzz of flies swarm in black masses trying to enter the barn. The two deputies give a silent, knowing look to each other as they enter into the doors of demise.

Yep, they found Melancholy Doom. He is hanging suspended from a rope slung over the high ceiling rafter. Maggots crawl haphazardly from his eye sockets, stripping his fleshy being in the sultry heat of the day. Rookies in law enforcement would possibly choke down the urge to vomit, but these two seasoned officers stand in amazement as they figure out how Melancholy got the rope over such a high rafter. After some debating and arguing, the deputies never reach an agreement about Melancholy's technique, so instead they start arguing whose call it is, trying to push the call off on the other one because of the high volume of paperwork and the death notification to the next of kin.

Finally, after a very long debate, Deputy On-my-way convinces Deputy Not-so-lucky it is his/her call and investigation.

As Deputy On-my-way clears the scene, he/she calls back to Deputy Not-so-lucky, "I'm just going to leave you hanging out with Mr. Melancholy," chuckling over the use of words.

To the streamline of society, this sense of humor may seem a bit harsh and perhaps even a little on the morbid side. But LEO has to be able to find a way past the horridness of the call in order to move on and survive investigating the woes of society. Calls such as these cannot become personal to LEO. It is not that LEO does not have a heart as big or bigger than the next person, it is just imperative LEO looks at the situation without becoming personally involved in order to survive emotionally as an officer.

When you live with LEO, stories such as this one are commonly shared among LEOs but suppressed when talking to the public. Most LEOs are very, very respectful to families of lost ones because they have seen the pain and suffering over and over numerous times; it burns in their hearts. While LEOs may appear callous with each other, they recognize personal tragedy and agony, carrying a heavy burden of sad, sad memories imbedded in their souls.

Do LEO supporters develop a harsh exterior from being associated with LEO? Perhaps, over time, we do. We may develop an insensitive way about us and not even realize it. It is my belief we develop a more calloused sense of viewing the travesties of society so that we too may emotionally survive law enforcement.

The charred body of a vagrant has been discovered on the edge of Seedy Lane. Upon investigation, the identity of the remains comes back to Rodney Raper. Apparently, Rodney Raper ran from neighboring law enforcement after raping two young girls, torturing them severely, beating them, and leaving them for dead. Because Rodney Raper wasn't the brightest in calculating the weather, he tried starting a fire to stay warm in the darkness of the freezing winter night with lighter fluid which unknown to Rodney Raper had spilled on his drunken body. Thus, when the match was lit, Rodney Raper went up in flames. (Justice well served.)

By the time the news media arrives, the responding law enforcement agents are drinking coffee and eating donuts near the charred remains in the early morning light. A photo of the officers is captured and splashed on the front of the local newspaper. Some in the administration of law enforcement may become concerned this photo gives the appearance of a cold, uncaring agency.

I wouldn't spend another second worrying about it. In my book, Rodney Raper got a small taste of what it's going to be like when he burns in hell for his sins.

So to answer the question about LEO supporters becoming calloused, yes, I guess we may acquire a bit of a hard shell being related to LEO.

CHASING FREEDOM

Many LEOs will become aware over time that it is best to try to leave Law Enforcement at the office when not on duty and focus on other outlets at home for the sake of sanity. Perhaps, LEO will take up a new hobby, coach sports, or want to start home improvements in order to be free for a few hours from the mistress of Law Enforcement. By now, the newness of the affair has worn off; although Law Enforcement is as enticing as ever, LEO is just so worn out from her demanding ways. LEO needs to seek solace and freedom by trying to concentrate on what other "normal" people do.

LEO starts exploring options of freedom. What do other "normal" people do? Normal people Facebook, Twitter, and MySpace. LEO says, "No, no, I don't think it is a very good idea for others to know when we are gone, etc. I don't feel comfortable with all this unlimited online information. All that is just like Christmas for those damn thieving criminals just waiting to steal or worse from poor unsuspecting victims."

Okay. What about watching television? Many "normal" people watch a tremendous amount of television.

The television is turned on and LEO flicks through the channels, one by one. While reality shows are very entertaining for mainstream society, the conflicts and drama are too much like being at work for LEO.

"Who wants to watch all that arguing and bitching?" LEO asks. "I see that at work. Don't people have better things to do?"

Finally, LEO turns the television to a channel with a reality law enforcement show. Huge mistake for LEO.

"What the hell is that officer doing? Did you see how bad his/her officer safety is? It's a wonder he/she has survived law enforcement this long if that is truly how they are out on the streets doing their job. My god!" LEO exclaims exasperated.

"They didn't even arrest that son of a bitch. Why the hell would you let that nasty, drug-infested perpetrator go? If I were their supervisor, they would have some explaining to do on that call," LEO continues.

To which you may gently suggest to LEO to turn the channel because apparently LEO's blood pressure is rising over the top. "Honey, surely something better is on. Let's see," as you take possession of the television clicker.

As you are trying to select a more calming, entertaining show, LEO does say, "*Wow*, did you see the fast patrol cars they have? I wish we had a few of those around. I bet they hit over 140 mph on hot calls."

Let's see. The next interesting channel is about gangs across America. Gang "lords," hierarchies, "turfs," and prison rivals are revealed in this true documentary. Murders and homicidal plots are examined as these gangs try for possession of our precious American youth and city streets. Graffiti, detailed gang tattoos, mob-like activities, and gangster violence are revealed. As you guessed, LEO gets wound up on a rampage of thoughts:

"I believe the American people should know about gang violence, but what gets me is the notoriety television shows like this give these little rat ass punks... Yada, yada, yada...need to infiltrate, put an end to drug supplies...Yada, yada, yada...need to isolate them in prison with absolutely no contact with other gang bangers...Yada, yada, yada..."

"Well, then," you remark, "let's see what else is on."

You calmly click the channel. The next interesting channel is about crime scene investigations. You chuckle silently to yourself as you know LEO will have a barrage of remarks about this one.

"We cannot afford to DNA test every crime scene. Do you know how much that would cost the taxpayers? And the way they show the crime happening early in the morning and by afternoon they have their suspect." LEO chuckles sarcastically. "Like that really happens. Yeah. Right."

LEO continues, "And the sad part is the public thinks we are letting them down if we don't try to get DNA samples from their yard when their pink plastic flamingos get stolen."

You silently chuckle. Yes, that is exactly the reaction you thought LEO would have.

Finally, you click to the weather channel. Surely there is nothing "work" related on the weather channel.

Wrong. A super cell of tornadoes has ripped through tornado alley. Coverage of the devastation is in full gear with emergency crews being dispatched to numerous communities. All are on alert. Sirens are blasting as all emergency personnel are heading toward the damaged communities.

LEO remarks, "I sure feel sorry for them. They didn't even have a chance." LEO hangs his head as he gets up off the couch and starts to leave the room.

"Where are you going?" you may ask.

"To reload bullets," LEO disappointingly answers.

BROADEN HORIZONS

As discussed in the previous chapter, LEO may desire to take up hobbies or work on home projects to gain freedom from LEO's law enforcement career when he/she is off duty. While this can be a very welcoming phase for LEO, beware that you may end up acquiring skills you never anticipated.

For example, LEO was in construction before his law enforcement career. LEO wants to add on to the existing house structure. Great. That will add an extra room for hobbies, an extra bathroom for the kids, and just be a great addition to the house. You are in.

LEO thinks as artistic as you are, you can draw house plans to cut back on the expense of having to pay for blueprints. *Wow.* You have never drawn blueprints before, but you study and study and feel prepared enough to try. While the kids are at school, you draw tediously, using many measuring templates you are not familiar with until you think you have an accurate blueprint with all the rooms of the house drawn in the correct scale of measurement.

LEO critically evaluates the blueprints, making quite a few changes. Once again, you are back at the drawing board while the house is quiet, concentrating on tediously reconstructing the design of the blueprints. LEO once again critically evaluates the blueprints. You are once more back to the drawing board making tedious corrections on the blueprints. By now, you are thinking, "How did I get suckered into this?"

LEO gives you his winning "I love you" smile as he tells you what a great job you did, and he thinks the plans are ready to be submitted to the building inspector for approval.

The plans are approved, and it is time to get started on the foundation of the addition. LEO decides the two of you can pour the concrete base for the foundation together. *Wow.* You have never helped pour a foundation before, but if LEO thinks it will be a way to "spend time together," you will help. LEO decides it will be best to mix the concrete in a cement mixer to save on cost. Okay. By the end of pouring the foundation, shoveling sand, gravel, and cement into a turning, churning vessel, you may think, "How did I get suckered into this?"

The years pass quickly, your children are graduating high school and college, and the foundation is still bare of a building. You have preached and preached to LEO about how strange this looks until LEO decides one day the two of you should "spend time together" once again and start working on the add-on. During the process expanding many, many years, you acquire the skills of nailing, using an electric skill saw, a drill, a square, a chalk line, etc., to erect the frame. Because LEO's time at work can sometimes be unpredictable, you may find once you have mastered a skill, you will become responsible for finishing the task at hand.

"And how did I get suckered into this?"

LEO gives you his winning "I love you" smile and asks enthusiastically if you are ready to put up the Sheetrock. LEO explains it will be time "spent together" if you and LEO put up the Sheetrock, tape and finish it, and it will save loads and loads of money.

"*Wow*. I have never put up Sheetrock before, but if it will help," you think to yourself.

After hours and hours of taping, mudding, and sanding, you begin to appreciate why construction workers get paid so much money. You are exhausted and feel like planning LEO's demise when you recognize you have done most of the sanding in the white, filthy, dusty building area. You think, "How in the hell did I get suckered into this?"

LEO gives you his brightest "I love you" smile and asks devotedly how you would like to start painting "whatever colors you like" in the new rooms.

Okay, I get it. Just hand me the paint brushes.

While your LEO may not be into constructing additions to your house, my recommendation is to beware. LEO will more than likely broaden your horizons and life skills with one hobby or another.

Caution! Caution! Watch out if your LEO is into reloading bullets. He/she may try to recruit you to help. The only reason I have dodged this chore so far is my LEO is scared I will put too much or too strong of gunpowder and blow something up. (Sometimes, it may serve you well to act a little dumb.)

LIVING UNDERCOVER WITH LEO

His eyes are as cold as blue steel. His long blond locks are pulled back haphazardly into a ponytail at the nap of his neck. An unkempt beard and mustache sport leftover food particles mangled here and there. The lines in his facial expression give the impression of forbidden danger and risk. His clothing is torn, tattered, and obviously stained with continual wear for a lengthy amount of time. As you near him, you smell a stench of rancid body odor from days and days of sweat, perhaps, mingled with stale cigarette smoke and an unknown rotten stink.

As you observe him from across the table, all you can think is "So this is the man I married."

Your LEO may decide as time passes to go into different components of law enforcement. If your LEO decides to go undercover, you may have a very similar character sitting across the breakfast table from you.

Undercover work for LEO is exhilarating yet very dangerous. Undercover agents are thrown into the wicked pits of society to catch drug dealers and suppliers who care not of human worth. These evil maggots feed off inflicting our young with dangerous drug addictions and prostitution to feed their drug addictions. Many drug dealers have addictions themselves; so it becomes imperative to hook new victims up with illicit drugs to supply their own maggot habits. Money, money, money is all that matters to these worms of humanity. Most big drug dealers have outstanding warrants and have already served time in the prison system. They carry very dangerous weapons because most do not ever want to serve time in prison again. Therefore, most big drug dealers have little to lose by engaging in deadly force with law enforcement.

How does law enforcement catch the drug dealers, the maggots of humanity? Sometimes, it is by supplying undercover agents who look and smell so much like the real maggots, it is hard to tell the difference.

If your LEO goes into the undercover component of law enforcement and drives a different vehicle up and down your drive at all hours, day and night, changing his looks often, maybe even resorting to wearing wigs, Mrs. Noseytoot, your neighbor will more than likely think you have a barrage of different boyfriends. You may even have a conversation like this:

"How's LEO? You doing all right? Sure have seen different people at your house lately. Everything okay?"

You recognize this is self-serving on Mrs. Noseytoot's part because she needs reassuring the neighborhood isn't going all to hell judging from the looks of Undercover LEO. And you? You are very limited as to what you can divulge and to whom.

Living with Undercover LEO is very, very challenging. Sometimes, you do not know where he is, who he is with, or when you will see him again. The question, "It's 10 o'clock, do you know where your kids are?" comes to mind; except with you, you are thinking, "It's 10 o'clock, do you know where your husband is?" No, you do not because Undercover LEO is working in a different area miles and miles away.

Everything is secret, secret, secret; and everyone is suspicious, suspicious, and suspicious. If Undercover LEO runs into one of his "undercover clients" by accident while you are with him, he will act as though he has never, ever seen you. You pick up on this extreme behavior; pretend you have never, ever seen him and dodge out of the situation as quickly as you possibly can. You may even exit in your car, circle the block a time or two, evaluate, and then decide if it is okay to return to pick him up. When at last you are united with Undercover LEO, he may appear tremendously nervous and extremely on edge because the very last thing Undercover LEO wants to do is put his family in jeopardy and harm's way.

Undercover LEO may even remark, "Man, that was close." Undercover LEO will be on edge for quite a few days after the incident, worrying if anyone or anything gave away the relationship you have with him.

During this time, you may begin to feel second class when Undercover LEO accompanies you in public places. For example, if you try to cash a check and have Undercover LEO standing nearby, you may need to show every form of identification you have ever possessed including your birth certificate, your mother's and father's birth certificate, your immunization records, your driver's license, etc. Undercover LEO plays his part so well most ordinary citizens find it hard to trust him.

You will get to see the back room of restaurants you have never seen before. If you like to sit at the front table, forget that; you will get to sit in the very, very back, if at all. On occasions, some restaurants will claim to be filled to capacity even though you visibly see empty tables.

Your relatives may be inclined to call 911 when they see Undercover LEO ringing the doorbell.

"Hurry, come quick. There is a very suspicious guy at my front door. Oh my god, he is ringing the doorbell. Hurry! Hurry!"

Your children may experience fallout from LEO's appearance as well. Parents of other children may not want Little Susie or Little Tommy to play at your house. Little Sprout may even hear another mother exclaim, "Little Sprout's mother seems okay, but what on earth happened to her dad?"

Heaven forbid if you take the photo Undercover LEO brought home of him decked out in camouflage with confiscated marijuana plants and unthinkingly place it on the living room mantle because Undercover LEO is so proud of the work accomplished. When Little Susie's mother comes to pick her up at your house because Little Susie has been playing with Little Sprout, she may appear very disgusted while looking at the photo and continue to grab Little Susie, exiting your house quickly, apparently appalled and without explanation. You are totally astonished at her actions and totally astonished you did not think of the consequences that could be associated with placing the photo on the mantle. You examine the photo closer; Undercover LEO is sporting a big handsome grin through all the facial hair, wearing a mud-splattered camouflaged outfit, hugging a cropping of marijuana plants towering seven to eight feet in the air in a desolated forest area. What's not to love? Yet you realize Little Susie's mother has not a clue what LEO does for a living, and you are grateful she is appalled by the photo.

By the time Undercover LEO decides it is time to go back on patrol, you are just as ready to see him clean shaven, neatly dressed, and smelling like Irish spring soap. When he first started undercover work, he still had a little hair left on the top of his head. You are not sure if it is the stress of undercover work or just a joke by Mother Nature, but LEO is completely bald on the top of his head after living this secretive life.

And Mrs. Noseytoot could not be happier. After LEO cleans up to patrol the streets again, she approaches him from across the way.

"LEO, is that you? Has that been you all this time running up and down the driveway in different cars with different hair? And to think I thought your wife had lots and lots of ugly boyfriends!" she exclaims.

Thanks, thanks a lot.

LIVING WITH A DARE OFFICER

Perhaps, one of the most rewarding times in LEO's career is when he/she is selected to teach DARE in the public school system. DARE originally started in elementary schools and middle schools with the slogan of Drug Abuse Resistance Education. In the later years, it has also encompassed "destructive decisions" resistance as well. Basically, this program is presented by law enforcement agencies in conjunction with public school districts to provide ways of equipping young children and the youth in the community ways of saying "no" when being approached to use illicit drugs or being involved in destructive behavior.

LEO will be walking with you in the park, and all of a sudden a rush of young kids flocks about him/her. They are energized and enthused talking and conversing with their DARE officer. Most DARE officers are in agreement that this program is very beneficial in establishing a great rapport between school children and law enforcement agencies.

The children will be required to meet certain criteria before they can graduate the DARE program, earning a DARE T-shirt. DARE graduations are thrilling and exciting for the young graduates. Many agencies have "Darin the Lion" to hand out graduation certificates, which many younger children find fascinating. "Darin the Lion" is a person, sometimes a law enforcement officer or law enforcement officer supporter wearing a heavy lion costume consisting of a furry body and a fuzzy, fuzzy head. According to people who have sported this costume, the costume is very burdensome and hot, hot, hot inside.

So if you are a LEO supporter, you may be approached by DARE LEO in such a manner:

"Hey, sweetie. How would you like to dress up like Darin the Lion tonight? Help me out with the DARE graduation? It will be like a date."

"A *date*!" Only a DARE LEO would consider dressing up in a hot lion costume handing out certificates like a "date." The "norm" of society considers a nice dinner and a movie with popcorn and treats a "date." But not to your DARE LEO; dressing up as Darin the Lion constitutes a "date."

And while you do not look forward to being hot and sweaty, you really don't mind helping LEO because of the spark of optimism it brings to these young influential faces.

Just some words of advice to DARE LEO: If you do not talk your supporter into wearing the lion costume and you, LEO, decide to wear the costume yourself, you may want to rethink speeding in your patrol vehicle wearing Darin's head through the photo radar in the neighboring town because it strikes you as being hysterically funny. While you may laugh and laugh at your very creative humor, your chief may not when he/she receives the speeding citation addressed to the agency. Who's *not laughing* now?

LIVING WITH A SPECIAL
RESPONSE TEAM RESPONDER

"Shots fired, repeat, shots fired, at 20 Gauge Shotgun Drive," the dispatcher's voice anxiously announces over the police radio. "Suspect is barricaded. Suspect is armed and very dangerous. Use extreme caution. There are small children reported to be in house. Hold for further info."

Many larger law enforcement agencies have opted to develop special teams to respond to highly dangerous calls or red alerts like this one. While the public is familiar with the phrase SWAT, other law enforcement agencies may name the highly trained responders SRT or Special Response Team. These highly trained officers spend hours and hours physically, emotionally, and strategically training for very dangerous threats on society like this call. Usually, the SRT or SWAT training is in addition to regular mandatory training.

Immediately, every member of the SRT is called to report to "command," which may consist of a highly equipped van or vehicle parked out of range of the shooter but near the dangerous situation. A commander then starts organizing and "briefing" SRT members as they arrive. SRT members wear specialized helmets, bulletproof vests, and more than likely are carrying automatic weapons and ballistic shields. Technology may also supply the agency with a highly specialized armored tank or even an entry robot.

Once the situation is scoped out, which usually takes only a few minutes because of highly skilled officers, a perimeter of SRT members is set up around the house located at 20 Gauge Shotgun Drive. This precaution allows no one in and no one out of the residence.

After perimeter is established, the neighborhood is very carefully and quietly evacuated by other law enforcement officers, never losing perimeter, as long as no threat is present to the evacuees. As long as the situation has not escalated, negotiations with the shooter will begin.

Negotiators may try calling the suspect. However, if the suspect will not answer or talk over the phone, a "black box" may be tossed into the residence to set up communication with the negotiator as long as it is safe to do so from an outside distance. The "black box" allows the negotiator to converse with the suspect and vice versa.

Negotiators are highly trained officers who have the endowment of defusing bad, bad situations through the gift of gab. Negotiators are very special individuals who can talk and talk and talk with the suspect about anything and all things, trying to defuse the perilous situation at hand. Negotiators may talk to the suspect about pizza:

"Hey, are you hungry? I can order you a pizza. What kind of pizza do you like? I like pepperoni with extra cheese. Do you like pepperoni with extra cheese? Because I can order you one and have it delivered. Do you like supreme? I like supreme pizza on Sundays when I watch football games. Do you like football games? My favorite team is the Denver Broncos. Do you have a favorite team? Did you see their last game…" Talk, talk, talk.

Even if the barricaded suspect does not answer the negotiator, the negotiator will continue talking, trying to gain the trust of the troubled individual. In this scenario, the focus of the SRT is to retrieve the children from the house unharmed, so it is hopeful the negotiator will be able to diffuse the tense standoff.

While LEOs ordinarily are impatient creatures, in these circumstances, SRT LEOs will be very, very patient for hours and hours as long as no shots are fired, trying to retrieve the children safely.

SRT LEOs are on the perimeter in "ready" mode as commanded by the commander; meaning if necessary, they are ready to storm the residence to take the suspect into custody if the situation starts to go sour.

The talkative and talented negotiator has been able to talk the barricaded subject into releasing the small children. To the relief of the SRT members, three small children run scared from the front door of the house.

Minutes turn to hours. Finally, the pressure of the talkative negotiator pays off and the suspect emerges, hands up, from the front of the residence. SRT members swarm quickly to secure the subject, face down, hands behind his back, placing handcuffs speedily.

It is at this point the SRT members are torn between treating the suspect as a threat and actually being sympathetic with his pitiful dilemma. As they turn him over to face him, they realize urine soaks the front of his dirty trousers. In a drunken, drug-provoked slur, the suspect cries, "I'm giving up. I'm fucking giving up. I can't stand it. I can't fucking stand it."

To which, SRT Member Entry One inquires, "Can't stand what?"

Tears stream down the suspect's face. "The voice. The fucking voice," he screams in a pitiful weep. "I couldn't find it. It just kept talking and talking. The voice," he bawls.

"I was going to shoot my fucking self, but when the voice just kept talking and talking, I got fucking scared," the suspect breaks down sobbing, trembling pathetically. "I was scared the fucking voice would follow me to fucking hell, talking about fucking pizza, family, and shit like that. So I'm giving up. Please, please help me. Please take away the fucking voice," he cries.

Officer Negotiator smiles a big smile. Thankfully, this one ended peacefully. As Officer Negotiator starts to approach the subject, the other SRT members motion for him to stand down, shaking their heads in a commanding motion of "Don't say a word!"

Officer Negotiator chuckles a little over this silent command, relieved the suspect released the children unharmed and the suspect will eventually be okay. The

SRT Commander walks up to Officer Negotiator on his way to the emotional suspect. He jokes, "I knew this guy was very serious when he listened to you for four and a half hours. Good god, that's just torture."

When you live with SRT LEO, he/she is ready to run to the highest level of danger anytime, anywhere. This is very noble and gallant; but it can also be very, very inconvenient for the family. For example, you and LEO have planned months and months for a once-in-a-lifetime vacation. You are packing the last few items in the car to head to the airport when SRT LEO's phone rings. It's a hot call. He scurries to get his gear and speeds away.

As LEO is driving away in a cloud of dust, you are running behind, yelling, "Are you coming back to go?"

You know in your heart it is very hard to answer the question. Maybe and maybe not.

You look despairingly at the kids who are clamoring with questions of their own. "Are we going to leave him? Are we going on vacation without him? Should we unpack his stuff? Do you think he will make it back in time?"

"I don't know," you say, not sure which question you are answering.

Time to leave for the airport. No SRT LEO. You are evaluating the situation. Should you just leave him and try to meet up with him later? Should you wait on him and all of you miss the plane?

Are you able to even think with "Mom, let's just leave him. He will find us. That's what he does for a living. He finds people. He will find us too"?

"We can't leave Dad. He wouldn't leave us. We all go or none of us go," proclaims Small Tot.

"Leave him," "Don't leave him" swirl in your brain.

Finally, tired of the arguing, you proclaim you will give SRT LEO ten minutes. If he is not back, you are going to leave him.

Nervously, everyone watches the clock. When nine and a half minutes pass, SRT LEO appears, cheerfully asking, "Okay, who's ready for vacation?"

In nine and a half minutes, you have counted every second the clock ticked—3,420 to be exact. You have stressed and fretted to the point of growing premature wrinkles, budding a streak of gray down the middle of your freshly dyed hair, and aging to the point of looking like SRT LEO's mother.

And LEO? Just happy as a lark, smiling, jumping in the packed vehicle, ready to go on vacation.

WHEN YOU ARE THE CRIMINAL

While I think the majority of civilian society tries to stay within the boundaries of the laws, there are occasions when even those of us who try very hard may unknowingly slip and disobey the law. Mind you, ignorance of the law is no excuse. If you slip, ever so slightly, and break the law, ever so minutely, LEO will never, ever let you live it down.

LEO is sleeping like a baby on the passenger side of the car, the seat laid back, snore, snore, snore, and you are driving to the best of your abilities. You navigate the two-lane road very, very well until you get into a construction zone. The van in front of you suddenly stops, indicating a right hand turn by signaling. There used to be a passing lane to the left, but due to the construction, it is gone. Your only chance of not ramming the van in front of you is to accelerate, passing on the right, passenger side of the van, quickly so the van will not hit your vehicle. You successfully complete this defensive driving maneuver to your satisfaction and astonishment. Thank God LEO is still heavily sleeping.

All is great. You are so proud of yourself. All is great until you realize a vehicle is approaching from behind with great speed and lights. What? Lights?

Yep. You are being stopped, pulled over by a law enforcement agent.

As you pull over, the gravel on the asphalt along with the declining speed wakes LEO. Groggily and accusingly, he asks, "What have you done?"

There is no time to explain. You are shaking like a leaf when Officer Traffic approaches asking you if you realized you passed the van on the turning side of "*his*" lane, which could have easily caused a collision, not to mention the acceleration of your vehicle could have endangered the situation to a higher degree. Stunned, you look at LEO who is looking at you in amazement, and *not good* amazement.

"I'm so sorry, Officer," you reply. "The last time I drove through this section, it was not under construction and there was a turn out lane for turning traffic, which there is not anymore because of the construction cones, and I was so shocked when I realized the van had stopped and was making a right turn, so to avoid hitting the van, I rammed on the gas to pass on his passenger side as fast as I could so I didn't hit him in the back, and he didn't hit me in the side, and I am very, very sorry," you ramble.

As you glance in LEO's direction, his expression has not changed—amazed, but not in a good way.

You reach cautiously across LEO to open the glove compartment. You notice his glare but proceed to hunt for what the officer requested: proof of registration and insurance, or was it proof of insurance and registration? Paper rattles as you hand over your proof of insurance and registration; you are trembling so badly. In a broken voice, you explain to the officer you are very, very sorry you are having trouble getting your driver's license out of your wallet because you are having trouble getting your wallet out of your purse because you are having trouble getting your purse out of the backseat, which he seems to have already noticed.

The officer sternly scrutinizes you as if he wonders of your sanity. He glances at LEO questioningly. Then he focuses back on you.

As you hand him all that he asked for, he quickly instructs, "Ma'am, just sit tight. I'll be right back."

You look in your rearview mirror. In the midst of the flashing lights, you see the silhouette of Officer Traffic, who appears to have the capabilities of beating a bear with a stick, conversing on his police radio. Because you live with LEO, you know the drill. He is running a check on your driver's license and tag number to assure you have no outstanding warrants, and your vehicle is correctly registered, not stolen.

In your nervous state, your mind wanders. Wouldn't it be funny if a mistake was made and the car came back stolen with you having multiple warrants? As you unconsciously smile because of your silent humor, you realize LEO is staring at you and does not find anything comical about the traffic stop.

"He ought to write you a ticket," LEO growls. "You know better. Were you trying to kill us? I would write you a ticket to the highest offense. Why if the van had speeded up during the turn and hit us in the side?"

You wittingly answer, "Well, it would have been my side if that is any consolation."

"He ought to write you a ticket," LEO continues. "He probably will write you a ticket. I write tickets for this all the time. I cite people for reckless driving for things less than this all the time. You are going to get a ticket for reckless driving. I believe it falls under Statute 473…yada, yada, yada. Our insurance is going to go up now because he is going to write you a ticket."

"SShhh, he's coming," you warn LEO.

You smile as Officer Traffic hands you back your driver's license, registration, and proof of insurance.

"Ma'am, I'm only giving you a warning citation today. Due to the construction zone, I can see where it could be confusing. However, I'm warning you, if I ever see you pass on the passenger's side of a turning vehicle, I will write you a hefty ticket. Is that clear?"

"Yes, sir," you acknowledge.

The officer continues, "Safety first." He looks at you to make sure you comprehend what he is telling you.

"Yes, sir, safety first," you repeat earnestly.

"The warning citation will not affect your insurance premium. You will not be required to pay a citation. It is simply warning you of a minor offense of unsafe lane usage, but it lets you know and my supervisors know I am working to keep the highways safe."

"Yes, sir."

"Please sign and date to acknowledge you received this warning citation."

"Yes, sir. Thank you, sir," you say as you shakingly try to write your name, trying to get your hand to stop trembling to carry out the deed.

Officer Traffic gives you a copy of your *warning* citation and says very politely, "Ma'am, have a nice day."

As you pull back out on the highway from the traffic stop, LEO scowlingly asks, "Do you want me to drive, or do you think you can use the correct lane to pass traffic? I just can't believe he didn't write you a *real* citation. What was he thinking? (Yada, yada, yada.)"

Perhaps, on another occasion, you try to use a personal check to purchase Christmas gifts. The clerk asks to see identification. You hand the clerk your driver's license. The clerk refuses to let you pay for the items with your personal check because *your driver's license is expired*.

"What? Expired?"

To your shock, the month is December and your license has been expired since May. Let's see. That's not just a few days, that's not just a few weeks, that's not even a couple of months. That's *eight* months. And your worse dilemma is not apologizing to the clerk for returning the Christmas items back to the shelves, it is not thinking of going to the motor vehicle department to obtain a current, legal driver's license, it is facing LEO.

"Honey," you say sweetly to LEO, "would you mind driving home?"

"Why? Are you sick?" he inquires.

You are thinking, "Not yet but probably by the time you get through with your lengthy, lengthy, lengthy lecture, I'm going to be." And you innocently explain about your expired license and how it could very easily happen to anyone.

"I write citations to people for *expired* license. How could you not notice it was *so expired*? Maybe a few days, maybe a few weeks, but months, *months*?" LEO rants.

Then you are faced with asking the worse question ever, "LEO, honey, will you take me first thing in the morning to MVD? I have a very busy week, and I really need my license to be legal."

"*Yes. I will.* I hope they make you take the actual written test and the driving test as well. I believe it is mandatory they do according to ARS Statute Number Such and Such, etc. If I were them, I would make you do all of it from beginning to end. I would make you take the written. I would make you drive." (Yada, yada, yada.)

"How many feet do you follow from the vehicle in front of you in a twenty-five-mile-an-hour zone? If you see a pedestrian crossing the street in a nonpedestrian zone, who has the right of way? How fast is the speed limit in a residential area?" LEO fires one question after another to see if he thinks you are capable of passing the driver's test since apparently you were not capable of knowing when your license expired.

LEO rants all the way to MVD the next morning, "I write citations for this. And it's a hefty fine. I write citations for this. And I think it is very important to possess a legal, current documentation for the right to drive…"

The motor vehicle clerk declares all you need to do is simply smile into the camera and pay the fee.

Yes! you think.

LEO butts in, "Doesn't she need to take the written test? Her license is very, very expired."

The clerk smiles sweetly at you and proclaims, "If it had been expired much longer, we would probably make her take it. But since it's only been a month or two, we can probably get by with her simply smiling in the camera and paying the fee."

Finally, someone on your side. To this day, that is the best picture you have ever, ever had on your driver's license.

WHEN A FAMILY MEMBER DECLARES THEY INTEND TO COMMIT A CRIME

LEOs are very honest, upstanding individuals. The integrity and commitment they have to obeying and enforcing the laws of the land is what sets them apart from being an ordinary citizen. It is my belief this strong allegiance and dedication will persevere even when someone close to them announces their intention of committing a crime.

How will LEO handle such a situation?

For example, Small Tot, LEO's son, is in third grade. Small Tot has declared numerous times his dislike for the playground teacher at school, Mrs. Uptight. Mrs. Uptight apparently criticizes the children in a constant and demeaning manner. Small Tot does not agree with her punishments. Small Tot believes she is so out of line when she enforces playground rules that she should not be allowed to be the supervisor.

LEO recognizes this is very uncharacteristic for Small Tot who usually respects authority. Therefore,

LEO gives merit to what Small Tot is telling him. There must be some harassment on Mrs. Uptight's part for Small Tot to feel the way he does.

Small Tot comes home very, very angry from school. Mrs. Uptight made him and his friend climb down from the very high monkey bars and sit on the bench all of recess because they were "talking and laughing too loud." Small Tot is irate because he feels recess is a time for talking and laughing loud.

Small Tot is so embarrassed and angry over the punishment, he declares, "I am going to climb high on the monkey bars, and when Mrs. Uptight walks under me, I am going to jump off on her and tackle her to the ground."

LEO is so surprised at Small Tot's outrage; however, he respects Small Tot's feelings. Mrs. Uptight has not been fair, but LEO warns Small Tot that jumping off the monkey bars and tackling her to the ground is not appropriate and could even be construed as an assault on a teacher.

Small Tot declares he doesn't care. "It is not fair how she treats us."

LEO talks to Small Tot about other options of solving the problem. Perhaps, scheduling a meeting with the principal will help.

Small Tot doesn't think this will help one bit because Mr. Strictness likes the way Mrs. Uptight is on the playground.

To LEO's dismay, he has very little success in convincing Small Tot there are other solutions to solving the playground quandary besides tackling Mrs. Uptight.

LEO threatens Small Tot, "I'm telling you once and for all, you better *not* do it."

Small Tot smiles while he pats LEO gently on the shoulder, never responding in regard to his intentions.

The next day as LEO is on duty, a call comes out over the police radio, "All units please respond to Edgy Elementary School. We have reports of a teacher being assaulted by a student."

LEO's heart sinks into the pit of his stomach. He warned Small Tot. He drives code with lights and siren to get there to find out the situation. His nerves are on edge, which is really unusual.

When he enters the principal's office, there is no way to express how relieved LEO is to find out it had absolutely nothing, nothing at all to do with Small Tot or Mrs. Uptight. Thank you, God. To LEO's realization, he has responded to dangerous domestic calls involving guns and multiple subjects in a more composed manner than responding to a call that could have involved his son.

The thought of hugging the principal is entertained for a second and then dispelled.

How do you spell relief?

Small Tot not tackling Mrs. Uptight.

WHEN DANGER LURKS
TOO CLOSE

His little beady dark eyes shift side to side. He is a calloused creature. He pauses in his tracks, calculating where he wants to go. He takes delight in knowing he is dangerous and feared by humankind. He has the power to instill fear. He slithers deviously to your back door.

There has been a massive manhunt in the area for a killer of the innocent. Radio, newspaper, and posters alert the community to be suspicious of anyone unfamiliar in the vicinity. The mass murderer apparently takes delight in torturing his victims before causing their horrid demise, decapitating and dismembering the bodies of the unfortunate. The killer does not act alone. Recently sprung from a maximum security prison, he has his two sons accompanying him on his slaughtering spree. Terror spreads rapidly; all are on the lookout for Slaughter Crimson and his boys.

You and the kids are tired from the day's activities. You arrive home from spending the day in the park and decide to have a relaxing evening watching TV and eating pizza while LEO is at work. The pizza has just been removed from the oven when your Doberman pincher, Assassin, growls a very low and threatening growl. He proceeds to bark ferociously as if warning you of danger.

What's up with Assassin? He never barks or growls. He never barks or growls unless there is something strange near.

He continues barking and barking, mixed with bloodcurdling growling. Your mind races wildly. Why if the killers have found your house? What is lurking near Assassin? By the time you call LEO, it could all be over with your head scattered at one end of the house and your arms and legs amputated at the other. And what of your poor innocent children?

Time to act. You secure the children under your bed, daring them to hardly move and to only breathe when necessary. You grab your .357 revolver from the safe place, check to be sure it's fully loaded, and grab the extra bullets, placing the box in your pocket. This job may call for reloading if necessary. Shakingly, you realize your dilemma. Because you are so nervous, you may have to shoot several times in order to stop all three intruders.

You pray, "Dear God, Please give me the presence of mind to shoot accurately and effectively. And, Dear God, please help me have nerves of steel if I need to reload. I ask You to please walk with me in this time of stress. Please save my children. In Jesus's name I pray. Amen."

"And, Dear God, if I have to shoot, help me to know when to stop so I don't keep reloading and shooting."

Now, for the task at hand. Although Assassin is ordinarily a very brave soul, he has continued barking as if frightened. You have peered from every visual point of the house to see nothing out of the ordinary. The way Assassin's pen is constructed, there is a blind spot. Therefore, you calculate the intruders are using this blind spot for their advantage.

With gun ready, you swing open the outside door closest to Assassin in the ready to fire position at which time you realize in your panic you forgot to call 911. Your cell phone is nowhere near. Crap. Maybe Mrs. Noseytoot will hear the shots fired.

The dog goes absolutely berserk when the door flings open. You carefully stay inside as much as possible while trying to scour the terrain where felons might hide.

To your astonishment, you see the intruder. It is not Slaughter Crimson and the gang. It is a Gila monster, ready to attack.

What? Are you seeing things? A Gila monster? This far north in the Mogollon Rim area of Arizona? Impossible, you think. Gila monsters are desert devils, very large slimy lizard like reptiles decorated with orange and black scales on their poisonous bodies sporting large mouths with smacking jaws to better chew poison into victims with numerous daggerlike teeth.

Assassin is ready to attack. You fear he will be the victim of a deadly bite, so you try to distract the distraught Doberman with pizza.

You stumble back in the house unsure what to do when the pizza runs out because Assassin is not going to leave the threat without a fight.

You call LEO. His first question as you watch this creature from hell foam and slap his powerful jaws together is "Honey, are you sure it isn't just a big lizard?"

"No. It's the creature from hell who is going to chew up Assassin, and you better get here as quick as you can," you hysterically reply.

LEO comes to secure the poisonous Gila monster. The Gila monster is a protected species in the state of Arizona. This fact alone is the only reason the Gila monster is still hissing; otherwise, you would have blown several holes in his scaly beady body just out of sheer fright.

LEO has the Gila monster "in custody" in a cardboard box. He checks in on his police radio, "P505."

To which the dispatcher responds, "P505."

"No assistance needed. I have a 10-15 (meaning prisoner). I'll be en route to the station. I'm Code 4 (meaning he is okay)."

All the pizza is gone. You forgot the kids are still under the bed. Assassin is very tired but okay. So all in all, everything is Code 4 now.

SOMEONE NEEDS TO BE CALM

Perhaps, one of the biggest emotional hurdles to overcome in life is when one of your children learns to drive. It is very difficult to distinguish if it is the prospect of independence that is so frightening or if it is the fact they may very easily kill someone or themselves. Living with LEO, you have heard every horrible horror story imaginable involving teen drivers.

While over the years you may have experienced times of being a nervous wreck living with LEO, none may compare to the times you try to teach your child to drive. And that in itself is your first challenge. If your "child" is old enough to drive, your offspring is *no longer* a "child" but a young adult with the emphasis being on "adult."

It is funny how life sometimes shows us a side of ourselves we do not even recognize. For example, Little Sprout has now bloomed into quite an attractive young intelligent lady, Sunflower Blossom, who is learning to drive the family vehicle (you paid an arm and a leg for) on the main highway. You try to trust her driving skills; you try to trust her visual abilities to see other vehicles and strive to avoid hitting them.

But somehow, in your personal growth, the trust just isn't there yet. You find you become extremely nervous, talking and jabbering, on and on, with beads of sweat pouring from every orifice of your body, soaking your clothes and the car seat. Jabber, jabber, jabber, you go, making little if any sense because you cannot control the panicky sense that has overtaken your mind and body.

"What is wrong with *you*?" Sunflower Blossom asks.

"Nothing, just enjoying riding with you," you lie.

"You aren't even making sense," Sunflower Blossom states as she takes her eyes off the road to survey why your side of the car appears so damp.

"Don't look at me! Don't look at me!" you scream. "Look at the road! You are going to kill us!"

Who is this maniac? You don't even recognize your own voice. Now, you have made Sunflower Blossom nervous too. In her nervous panic, she plows her foot on the gas pedal, weaving in and out of slower vehicles, barely missing here and there, not really sure how to pull out of the crazy panic she is in.

And for once, you are totally frightened to the point of being totally speechless. Words form in your mind but will not come out of your mouth. She looks to you for advice and reassurance, and you are fidgeting silently, in the state of terror, and absolutely no help at all.

Miraculously, she regains her composure enough to slam on the brakes in the high school parking lot, squealing tires due to the impact of the stop. You whisper you love her. You try to tell her to have a good day. She shakes her head in a disappointing stare and stomps off to class.

Are you able to drive home? You don't know.

Will LEO be better at this than you? That is the question.

Yes, LEO is tremendously better at this than you are to the point of envy.

Same scenario. Sunflower Blossom is driving the vehicle (you paid and arm and a leg for) on the main highway to school. LEO is instructing from the passenger side, and you have been placed in the backseat with strict instructions to remain quiet regardless the circumstances. After last time, you readily agree to the stipulations placed on your communications with Sunflower Blossom by LEO.

"Do not talk to her. Do not scream at her. If she needs you to talk, then you talk to her," LEO instructs.

"Clear, got it," you reply, confused whether to talk or not, but knowing better than to ask.

Sunflower Blossom cheerfully chatters to LEO about the upcoming dance, the volleyball game, how cute one of the football players is seeming not to notice the semitruck stopping at the red light in front of her. You are seconds and inches from having a nasty, nasty accident.

As you hear someone screaming hysterically and realize it is you, you also hear LEO's calming voice, "Sunflower Blossom, if you do not apply pressure and a significant amount of pressure to the brake pedal right now, we are going to plow through the backend of the semitruck stopped in front of us." He never raises the pitch of his voice—just calm, calm, and calm.

To your utter amazement, Sunflower Blossom stops the car on a dime within two inches of ramming with great force the truck in front of her. She smiles over at LEO, and he smiles at her.

Very calmly again he proclaims, "Good job!" as if instructing her on how to cut carrots or some task not life threatening. Then he peers behind him at you in the backseat. He gives you a wink that says, "This is how it is done."

In this pivotal time, you realize it is LEO's training in his/her law enforcement career that gives him/her the strength, the courage, and the wisdom to remain calm. And to that, you are very, very thankful and very, very quiet.

LEO, REACTING TO A CHANGING WORLD

L EO sits in the living room, gun kit strewn all over the top of the coffee table with rifles, shotguns, and duty weapons stacked and laid all over the place.

"What are you doing?" you ask in an irritated tone and continue, "Sunflower Blossom's date is going to be here any minute, and you knew that. What did you do? Pull out every gun you own? What's her date, Jumpy One, going to think?"

LEO sits back on the couch, grinning with self satisfaction.

"Now, wonder what Jumpy One might think? Wonder if I really care what Jumpy One thinks?"

You give LEO a disapproving look as there is a knock at the door.

"That's him. Can't you clean some of this up?" you plead.

LEO shakes his head "no," smiling, very content with himself.

"Jumpy One, how nice to see you. Won't you come on in? Sorry for the mess. LEO decided to clean his duty weapon," you apologize calmly as you see the shocked look on Jumpy One's face as he surveys the large arsenal of guns in the room.

"You shoot guns?" LEO asks him in a gruff tone.

Jumpy One is so nervous; he finally shakes his head "no," trying to smile.

"That's too bad," LEO states as he picks up a long-barreled rifle. "Nothing quite like the feel of a good quality gun discharging a lethal round into a scoped out target." He winks.

You chime in trying to redirect the conversation. "Here, let me move a few guns and make some room on the couch for you to sit down by LEO. Jumpy One, may I get you something to drink? Sunflower Blossom is upstairs getting ready, but she should be right down." You smile.

Jumpy One squeezes as far away from LEO as possible, almost sitting on the arm of the couch.

"No, I'm fine," he stutters as he looks curiously at LEO.

LEO catches his stare. This seems to delight LEO to no end. He returns the stare and proceeds with his interrogation questions.

"Where were you born? What month? What day? Do you play sports? What are your interests? Yada, yada, yada…"

LEO continues the questioning, becoming louder in volume when Jumpy One doesn't have an answer.

"What do you mean you don't know where your Great Aunt Lucille was born?"

Finally, Sunflower Blossom enters the room, looking absolutely beautiful, gaining the smiles of all.

"You look beautiful," LEO states emotionally.

"Thanks," she replies sweetly. "I'll be home at 11:00 pm. I won't be late. We will proceed directly to the dance. We will not detour or alter the quickest route to the dance. We will be at the dance the whole time I am gone. I will not leave the dance under any circumstances. Jumpy One will bring me home, directly home, with only me and him in the car from the dance on the shortest route possible. Jumpy One will not stop under any circumstances, not even if he has a flat tire. If he has a flat tire, we will continue to travel in this direction, calling you to assist us until we see you in view," she continues.

"Have a good time, honey," LEO says endearingly. LEO scrutinizes Jumpy One upon departure. He gruffly adds, "You, too, Jumpy One."

As they are leaving out of earshot, LEO turns to you and says, "I think he really likes me, don't you?"

"Yes, I think you are his favorite," you mock.

LEO kids may find adolescence more difficult than others. What parental LEO may not be able to watch, LEO's peers may be able to see on duty.

Think of Sunflower Blossom's surprise when she enters the house at 10:50 p.m. from the dance and LEO questions her:

"Why did you and Jumpy One go to the snack machines outside the dance? Were you really that thirsty for a Coke? Why did you buy three Butterfingers instead of two?"

Think of LEO's surprise when Sunflower Blossom answers, "That wasn't me, that was Jenetta. She wore a dress just like mine. Isn't that funny?" she sniggers.

WHO'S THE BOSS?

There are many, many occasions in a law enforcement officer's career when he/she may travel away from home for training. Usually, these training sessions last a week or two, but as your LEO climbs closer to the administrative level, he/she may be sent to longer training sessions such as the FBI Academy, which lasts three months.

When this happens, you will be left to take care of *everything*: the kids, the house, the vehicles, the pets, the lawn, etc. You may opt to fill notebooks (many, many notebooks) full of notes about what to do in a variety of instances.

For instance, if the hot water heater quits working, what will you do?

A. Sit and cry next to it, hoping it will eventually start working again.

B. Tell your kids it is healthy to shower in very cold water during winter because it will toughen up their immune system.

C. Go out for ice cream and try to forget about it.

D. Call Mr. Ex-plumber because he will be able to help you at a discount rate.

If you answered D, you are absolutely correct.

If the family car breaks down in a busy intersection, you should?

A. Pop the hood, grab a magazine out of the backseat to read, and sit on the trunk hoping your neighbor will come by.

B. Call your mother who lives two thousand miles away, crying pathetically.

C. Call your automobile insurance company to see if towing is included on your policy.

D. Stand in the middle of the intersection close to your vehicle, directing traffic while holding white Kleenexes hoping drivers will see you.

If you answered C, you are absolutely correct.

You are responsible for overseeing Sunflower Blossom's dating regiment. You should?

A. Pass this responsibility down to her younger brother.

B. Advise her she is not allowed to date until LEO returns and she is forty-four years old.

C. Always ask her date if you can go too.

D. Grab her sobbing uncontrollably, begging her to stay home with you.

If you answered A, you are absolutely correct. This plan works wonders to the amazement of many.

For example, as LEO is tearfully saying good-bye at the gate of the airport, getting ready to depart for the FBI academy in Quantico, Virginia, he looks down at your eleven-year-old son, Small Tot, who has now grown up into Vibrant Spirit.

LEO pats Vibrant Spirit on the top of his head proclaiming, "While I'm gone, you are the man of the house." LEO winks at you with a loving grin before kissing you good-bye and hugging Sunflower Blossom.

Could LEO have created a bigger mess than this?

Vibrant Spirit totally takes LEO at his word. The eleven-year-old is totally convinced he is the "Man of the House," and he believes he is the boss because LEO told him so.

Have you ever had an eleven-year-old tell you how inapt you are at vacuuming? Have you ever had an eleven-year-old plan a weekend of yard work and washing the car? Have you ever had an eleven-year-old tell you and Sunflower Blossom to quit laughing at the girly show on TV "and get busy doing something"?

Wow. If you could just strangle LEO right now who is thousands of miles away, you would feel so much *better*.

Your saving grace is this little eleven-year-old tyrant has also taken over supervising Sunflower Blossom's dating schedule. Vibrant Spirit knows when his sister, Sunflower Blossom, is to be home. If she is five minutes late, he is pacing up and down the floor, demanding, "Where is she, Mom?"

To your amazement, as her punishment, Vibrant Spirit insists she watch all of the *Jaws* movies with him because it is a *Jaws* marathon weekend. Sunflower Blossom takes the punishment harder than you would have ever, ever imagined. Not bad, you think.

Because Vibrant Spirit is truly LEO's son, he decides to creatively build a tree house so he can fortify your house by creating a "lookout" for strangers. After hours and hours of him directing you on how to nail this board and that board, you finally hammer in the last nail to his satisfaction. Vibrant Spirit takes a small fold-up chair, his BB gun, binoculars, peanut butter and jelly sandwiches (you made him) up in his tree house "fort" so he can "guard the place."

You are thankful. This will keep him busy enough to give you some *relief*, you think as you go inside.

Not so fast. You hear shouting downstairs. You rush to see what the conflict is. Sunflower Blossom is shouting at Vibrant Spirit, "Don't you ever, ever do that again! I will never, ever live down this embarrassment at school. How could you do this?"

"What did Vibrant Spirit do?" you inquire, puzzled over the commotion.

In his defense, Vibrant Spirit keeps repeating in a very loud voice, "I told you I don't like Scummy Pants. I told you I don't like Scummy Pants, and Dad doesn't like him either."

"What is going on?" you demand.

Sunflower Blossom explains, "Scummy Pants was bringing me home from our picnic. We were walking to the house when we saw Vibrant Spirit up in his 'fort' holding his BB gun. Well, Scummy Pants wants to be nice, so he said we should go say hi. We get up to the shack in the tree, Vibrant Spirit calls his 'fort' and Scummy Pants politely asks, 'What are you doing up there?'"

She continues irritated immensely, "And do you know what he said? Do you know what he said? He tells Scummy Pants someday he will have a shotgun instead of a BB gun. Scummy Pants was afraid to walk the rest of the way to the house because he thought Vibrant Spirit would shoot him full of BBs." She sobs. "I can't believe this has happened. He will never, ever come back!" She glares dramatically down at her eleven-year-old brother.

Defensively, Vibrant Spirit explains he never threatened Scummy Pants. Vibrant Spirit continues explaining how he doesn't think Scummy Pants has "honorable intentions."

"Honorable intentions?" *Wow*. Where did Vibrant Spirit hear that? That really does sound like LEO.

You are finally able to cheer Sunflower Blossom up by promising she can get three piercings in her left ear. (For now, you are just trying to survive until LEO gets home.) And when LEO does come home, all are overjoyed he is finally back until it is decision-making time. You think you should be boss, LEO thinks he should be boss, and Vibrant Spirit knows he *is the boss*.

ACCEPTING A HELPING HAND

B ecause LEO children are exposed to the criminal element on a daily basis, they too become suspicious of others. This is a good thing. This may someday save their lives. Because of the nature of their upbringing, they may also become acutely aware of someone needing help or being in distress. This is a good thing also. This is the spark of mankind to which all of us need to be more attuned. But does this present a problem for LEO?

Vibrant Spirit, your son, is now a very energetic thirteen-year-old. He is a very rambunctious young fellow, exploring his world, craving all the entertainment it has to offer in good and solid ways. As Vibrant Spirit is hiking the trail leading into the forest, he notices an abandoned vehicle rolled down a one-hundred-and-eighty-foot embankment. What if someone is still in there? This calls for a call to LEO.

LEO dispatches many branches of the agency assist personnel, including fire and ambulance. Upon arrival, crews of emergency workers and a huge crane is called to help lift the vehicle from the steep canyon. Funny no one noticed it before, but apparently, the vehicle had rolled to the bottom quite some time ago, perhaps thirty or forty years prior. Amazingly no one noticed it before! Before Vibrant Spirit. No skeletons remain in the vehicle, which means it was more than likely just abandoned by rolling it over the cliff.

LEO sends the initial responders on their way, back to the station.

"Whew!" Vibrant Spirit exclaims to LEO. "I'm glad that is all it is."

Vibrant Spirit decides to "hang out" at the park with some of his buddies rollerblading. As he is rollerblading down a very, very steep incline at about 50 mph, he notices a suspicious suspect with binoculars watching smaller children playing on the playground. Doesn't seem right at all to Vibrant Spirit. The suspicious suspect is wearing camouflage, concentrating on the small subjects, unaware Vibrant Spirit has spotted him. This calls for a call to LEO.

A team of officers is called to scope out the suspicious individual. After establishing a perimeter, LEO decides to make contact with the suspect to see if he is a pervert waiting for an opportunity to prey on young victims. After initial contact, LEO establishes the aging man, Wren Bluejay, is an avid bird-watcher and expert. He is watching a quail hen and babies, running in and out of a cropping of rocks, hoping to gain enough insight and material to publish his next article, Running Quail, in National Bird Magazine. Wren Bluejay did not notice there were little children in the park. Because of LEO's finesse in handling the situation, both LEO and Wren Bluejay chuckle a little; and because Wren Bluejay sees where others, especially parents, might become concerned, he offers to relocate to study the quail.

LEO 10-22s (cancels) the surrounding officers.

"Whew!" Vibrant Spirit exclaims to LEO. "I'm glad that is all it is."

Vibrant Spirit decides to ride his bike down the neighborhood street. He sees a very elderly lady limping step by step with a cane and seemingly having a great amount of difficulty. As he passes her, he notices her face is scrunched in pain. Vibrant Spirit decides to see if he can help. Mrs. Fartie Hardy is visiting her daughter. Her daughter went to work, forgetting to take her to her doctor's appointment. Because Mrs. Fartie Hardy needs a prescription refill, the elderly geriatric woman decided to just walk.

Just walk? It is a mile or more to the doctor's office. Vibrant Spirit does not think this is very good for Mrs. Fartie Hardy. She can't walk that far. This calls for a call to LEO.

LEO talks with Vibrant Spirit, and LEO assures him he will give her a ride. LEO is also thinking this will be a great opportunity to check and make sure Mrs. Fartie Hardy is not missing from a care facility. As he approaches the sidewalk where Vibrant Spirit and Mrs. Fartie Hardy are conversing, he notices how far away Vibrant Spirit is standing from the aged, wrinkled form of Mrs. Fartie Hardy. Because of LEO's expert training, he considers this a clue but is clueless as to why.

Until, he opens his patrol car. The worse smell *ever* permeates the air apparently coming from the poor fragile Mrs. Fartie Hardy.

Vibrant Spirit beams as he says, "Thanks, Dad. I just thought she really needed help." Smirking, Vibrant Spirit rides away quickly.

Mrs. Fartie Hardy cannot thank LEO enough for his compassion as he opens the door of his patrol car to let the little stinky lady in. He verifies Mrs. Fartie Hardy is not missing from a care facility and tries to resume taking her to her doctor.

But the smell. His gagging reflex takes over. He swallows down upchuck trying to maintain his professionalism. He rolls down all the windows of the vehicle, cranks the vent blower on high, and holds his breath, trying not to smell when he breathes in. He is empathetic with Mrs. Fartie Hardy realizing someday he will be old too but *the smell.* Gag, gag, gag.

She talks sweetly to him all the way to her doctor; her fragile white hair blowing crazy in the wind. He can hardly hear her over the noise of the blustery air blowing through the car and the vent blower on high. He shakes his head as if he is taking in every word she says.

He thinks of running code with siren and lights to get there quicker but quickly dismisses the idea when he thinks of the policies he would be breaking. He decides to opt for driving five miles an hour over the speed limit, swallowing the upchuck of his lunch, thinking about the fine mess Vibrant Spirit has gotten him into this time. LEO's memory of Vibrant Spirit standing afar from Mrs. Fartie Hardy conjures up the emotion of anger in LEO. Vibrant Spirit knew poor Mrs. Fartie Hardy smelled putrid and that LEO would be cooped up with her in his patrol car. The image of Vibrant Spirit finding humor in the situation conjures up even more anger in LEO.

Finally, LEO and Mrs. Fartie Hardy reach the doctor's office. As LEO looks at the pitiful woman, his anger with Vibrant Spirit fades. LEO recognizes he was just trying to do a good deed. LEO jumps out of his patrol unit, walks very quickly to his passenger side, and assists Mrs. Fartie Hardy out of the vehicle. To his shock, Mrs. Fartie Hardy hugs him in a tight, hardy embrace, tearily thanking him for his unselfish kindness.

What? As Mrs. Fartie Hardy walks *briskly* away without the use of her cane, LEO feels a wet, icky feeling on the front of his uniform pants. Apparently, Mrs. Fartie Hardy peed herself, and when she hugged him, the wetness soaked through on his uniform. Crap.

Crap. What about his passenger seat? As he sticks his head into the rancid, stinky car, he sees a huge wet spot where Mrs. Fartie Hardy had just sat. Crap. Now, his patrol car is drenched with pee, and the stink is pukingly unbearable.

LEO isn't going to let Vibrant Spirit get away with this one. In the heat of the moment, LEO decides to call him to let him know there is pee on his patrol car seat. Crap.

LEO shouts into the phone, "And she peed on my seat! And she hugged me, and now I have pee on the front of my uniform!"

"Whew!" Vibrant Spirit exclaims to LEO. "I'm glad that's all it is."

COPING WITH BEING A VICTIM

While visiting the big city, you decide to go to the mall to buy LEO shoes. LEO and you have shopped at the mall *all* day to find suitable dress shoes for LEO. LEO is not a very patient shopper. LEO does not like shopping for shoes. LEO thinks shoes are too, too expensive. LEO wants to be outside in the sunshine and *not* shopping for shoes. Whine, whine, and whine. You have had more enjoyable shopping trips with little tiny kids going through the terrible twos.

The shoes are too tight. The shoes are too dressy. The shoes are not dressy enough. LEO likes the color but not the style. LEO likes the style but not the color. LEO is driving you *crazy*. You finally reach your limit of tolerance and proclaim to LEO you are going to buy him the brown leather shoes with the square toes because that is just the best purchase to make.

"But I don't like them. I'm not going to wear them. I don't care if they do match all my dress clothes. I don't like the color brown they are. The square toes are ugly...yada, yada, yada," LEO goes on and on.

"You need dress shoes by Monday, and this is the best we can do," you hiss as you pull out your credit card to give to the clerk.

Whine, whine, whine.

You toss the purchase in the trunk of the car. Finally! You are ready to leave the mall.

Tired and exhausted from your day of shopping, LEO and you approach the building where your overnight accommodations are. LEO carefully selects the appropriate parking place because he, as usual, is very aware of the criminal element lurking everywhere. He decides to park in a well-lit parking place. It is under the streetlight, it is in full view of the check-in office, and it is in full view of passing traffic. Because you are toting your overnight bag, you decide to leave your laptop computer in the trunk, along with those stylish shoes you purchased for LEO. At the last minute, you decide to grab your purse and take it inside with you.

After a very enjoyable night, LEO and you are ready to load up and head home. Carrying your overnight bags, you walk to the car.

What car? Where is the car?

"I'm sure we parked here," LEO says.

After scouring the parking lot and the parking lots next to it and the parking lots next to them, you agree on the obvious: Someone *has stolen* your car; *your car* that you drive all the time.

LEO calls local law enforcement to make the stolen vehicle report. They will arrive shortly. As you wait for their arrival, LEO scratches his head as if very confused.

You are curious, so you ask, "What are you thinking?"

"Who would steal your car?" LEO says. "If I was a criminal and I knew I stood a chance of going to prison for auto theft, I would at least steal a better car than yours. Some criminals are just dumb."

That makes you feel so much better knowing a *dumb* criminal stole your car.

As the police report is being made, the officers inquire as to the contents left in the car. LEO tells them about the laptop computer, various tools, and the very *ugly* brand-new shoes you just bought him. The officers tell you how fortunate it is you decided to take your purse from the vehicle. If the criminals had gotten their evil hands on the credit cards, the identification cards, and the checkbook in your purse, the next few weeks and months perhaps would have became very, very challenging especially considering the identity theft crisis in the city.

LEO becomes very, very concerned when he realizes two of his guns were left in the vehicle. The police officers promise to place the guns in the computer system, so if found, LEO will be notified. His main concern is the criminals will use his guns to shoot an innocent soul, and LEO worries.

Upon renting a replacement car supplied by your insurance company, the clerk inquires to LEO's occupation. The rental car clerk simply cannot hide his amusement that a law enforcement officer's personal car is stolen. Then he states, "Shit happens everywhere."

LEO says with conviction, "Yes, it does."

On your way home, you share how violated you feel having *your* car stolen. "Those damn criminals. Those damn *dumb* criminals!" you vent to LEO.

LEO brings out positive points about the crime: At least you were not harmed, the car was not carjacked with you in it, and material things are always replaceable but people are not. Things could have been worse.

Then LEO starts chuckling, and says, "Some poor dumb ass is wearing the ugliest brown leather squared-toed shoes he has ever seen in his life because he wasn't smart enough to steal a different car; and his wife just thinks they look *'terrific'* on him."

Now, you really feel violated. You realize you have to go shoe shopping with LEO again.

WHERE DANGER BREEDS

If you have lived with LEO very long, you have been exposed to his/her genetic trait of being a magnet to danger and/or the criminal element due to the law enforcement syndrome. Experts have examined LEO's attraction to "cleaning up" the criminal element but have yet to explain the abnormity. One study focuses specifically on the "magnet theory," claiming it is positive/negative metal attractions, which magnetize LEOs to crime, but since have theorized it could also be primarily a mental defect (which LEO supporters already know). Upon investigating, it is obvious to even the most simple of minds that LEOs do not possess a *physical* condition with a makeup of positive metal ions attracted to the *physical* negative metal ions of the seedy, scandalous sectors of society. So why is LEO so magnetized to crime? It is my belief these ions are not physical components one can view under a microscope but instead are invisible magnetic attractions.

Consider the following example: LEO romantically decides to fly you to the San Francisco vicinity on Valentine's Day because LEO wants to take you to the

Legion of Honor and the de Young museums. He has planned this trip just for you to show you the beautiful paintings of the Old Masters and the relic, unique displays in the museums.

And you? You are in *total* shock. You weren't even aware LEO knew of such museums. You find this gesture on LEO's part to be one of the most romantic adventures anyone could have possibly imagined. And to think LEO imagined it. *Wow* you just love this guy!

The excitement of the trip is beyond description. The plan is to fly into Oakland on Valentine's Day and then spend the next three days taking in the sights of San Francisco. It seems like a *dream*, like just the best dream ever.

Your flight from Phoenix to Oakland is uneventful. LEO secures the rental car just fine, and you arrive at the hotel without any exposure to the criminal element. Check in at the hotel seems fine.

Then, LEO carries the luggage into the hotel elevator where you and LEO will travel up four stories to your hotel room. LEO and you are laughing and giggling with the anticipation of your Valentine's get away when LEO notices someone trying to stop the elevator door from closing. LEO gallantly saves the moment by pressing the open button.

What? Close it. Close it quick, you think. But it is too late. LEO and you squeeze tightly into the corner of the elevator to let the poster child gangster for Gangland and his girlfriend enter the limited space. Nervous, you are behind them; both "gangsters" squeeze their way to be directly beside of you so they can "size" you up. *Great*, you think. *We are going to die in an elevator in Oakland, stabbed or shot by a couple of strange gangbangers.*

As the 6'4", male gangster stares curiously at LEO; you cannot help but stare at him. He has dark, bloodshot, malicious eyes. His face has a few days growth of whiskers, which accent his cropped hair and his baseball cap turned backwards. Earrings protrude from his ears and his eyebrows. You fear the tattooed tear drops at each eye might possibly represent his dead rivals which he conquered. You are pretty sure the tats on his neck are symbolic of the gang he is affiliated with. He has chains dangling from all over his clothing, and you pray his sagging britches will stay up on his body until you descend from the elevator; that is, if you are lucky enough to descend from the elevator.

He continues to analyze LEO, studying LEO intently. More than likely, you suspect, he also knows LEO is affiliated with law enforcement just by LEO's demeanor .This reality isn't helping the tight space of the elevator feel any bigger. The gangster shifts his weight, rubbing a hand over the last teardrop on his face as if to draw attention to it. Great.

His chick (girlfriend) shifts a little. She too is somewhat sporty with multiple gang tattoos and piercings. The gang chick gives you a glance that says she can tear a grizzly bear apart with her bare hands within seconds. Okay, time to start praying.

As Gangbanger Danger places his arm over the shoulder of Gangbanger Chick, both you and LEO alert to his movement. Then, Gangbanger Danger smiles with an evil twist on his face.

"Hey, man, you having a good Valentine's Day?" he asks in a friendly sort of way.

Surprised, to the point you thought you might have to physically lift LEO up off the floor, LEO smiles back and says, "Yes, we are having a very nice Valentine's Day. What about you?"

"Yeah, man, it's great," he proclaims as he squeezes Gangbanger Chick closer to him, licking her cheek. The elevator stops. He smiles as the two of them exit as one onto their hotel floor.

All right then.

LEO smiles at you reassuringly. "This is going to be a great trip." He beams.

The museums are great. LEO is a great sport. You realize looking at paintings in museums isn't exactly LEO's cup of tea, but he is very patient and attentive while you look. You are not surprised that his favorite display is the display of *real* human skulls, which headhunters shrunk down to size in the primitive times of the Americas. He also points out to you how they used human bones in making tools and ornaments. LEO thinks the primitive natives were very imaginative and creative. Yes, they were; you agree.

LEO has reserved an afternoon for sightseeing the suburbs of San Francisco. You see no harm in this until LEO finds the most crime-infested city you have ever, ever seen. All the windows and doors, even on public buildings, are barred with steel and locks to keep the criminals out, which from what you can estimate is most likely every individual in the city.

You start getting nervous, but LEO isn't nervous. LEO is scoping out the criminal element as if in seventh heaven. He is like an avid fisherman in a lake over running with trout. He is like a kid in a candy store.

"Man, just think of all the arrests you could make in one night! *Wow*! And for all kinds of crimes! Why just look! I bet they are dealing dope right here on this corner. If we park, I bet we can watch," he says enthusiastically. He tries persuading you to be more excited about sightseeing the forbidden neighborhoods of the dangerous, perilous city.

By now LEO and you have attracted a few people interested in *you* and why *you* are in the neighborhood. You express your concerns to LEO.

As you survey a group of malicious-looking "homeys" lining up along the dirty street to get a better look at LEO and you, LEO inquires sarcastically, "You don't think they are just the friendly neighborhood greeters, the welcoming committee?" LEO laughs, amused with his sense of humor.

"*No*, I want to get the hell out of here. Why is it you always find the very worst places to go?" you accusingly ask in a voice you do not recognize. You unconsciously turn ashen white because the fear factor is beginning to take hold of your whole body. For some reason, you are trembling like a leaf in a ferocious wind, and you can't stop. You fear this could be the last few minutes you live.

You look hateful at LEO. LEO isn't worried. LEO apparently thinks he is going to live forever in the evil city because while you are jittering like a striped-assed ape in a den of hungry lions, LEO is very, very calm.

LEO explains innocently, "I don't know why I always end up in the worst part of town where danger breeds. I just know I like seeing what other places deal with in regards to crime. Makes me feel good about where we live. When I see a place like this, I just want to clean it up."

"Well, it makes me want to get the hell out of here," you say in a cranky voice as you see the number of "neighborhood greeters" growing.

LEO looks at the gathering in the foreboding neighborhood and agrees it is time to leave. You have worn out your welcome.

LEO starts making tracks away from the tense situation to which you are grateful. But to your absolute amazement as you pass a taco stand, boarded up tight with steel cages and locks on the windows, LEO has the nerve to ask you, "Hey, honey, you want a taco? I'm hungry. Bet this place makes the best tacos ever."

No thanks!

QUIRKY TRAITS OF LEO

"**Y**ou only love me because I am convenient," LEO says lovingly.

Funny, you have thought of LEO with many, many different adjectives; and to your recollection, "convenient" has never, ever been one of them.

Why does LEO think he is convenient?

A. LEO enthusiastically gets home on time even if he/she knows you are fixing shepherd's pie for dinner, which he/she hates.

B. LEO eagerly gets home on time even if he/she knows there is going to be a houseful of relatives or friends which he/she hates.

C. LEO does not volunteer for extra shifts while you are painting the outside of the house.

D. LEO only eats lunch meat and cheese on his/her sandwich therefore making life with LEO very convenient.

If you guessed D, you are absolutely correct. Life with LEO is so very, very convenient because he/she eats only lunch meat and cheese on sandwiches. You do not have to worry about mayonnaise, mustard, lettuce, and tomatoes, which is what most normal people eat. Your LEO is more convenient than that.

Let's explore the other choices:

A. If LEO knows you are fixing shepherd's pie, LEO will get home very, very late from a call requiring he/she "grab" something for dinner or will get called out unexpectedly if you have "leftover" shepherd's pie. You may even hear LEO stumble and call it "shitty" pie.

B. If LEO knows there are multiple relatives or friends of which he/she is not particularly fond in your house, he/she will ultimately get the "case from hell" at work, which he/she must investigate for hours and hours and days and days until all the "suspects are interviewed" (or until your visitors go home).

C. LEO will volunteer to chase down port-a-potty thieves before he/she will volunteer to pick up the ole paintbrush.

"I don't know why you think I am so stubborn."

Funny, sometimes the only description you can think for LEO is "stubborn." Let's look at some of the options as to why LEO thinks he/she is *not* stubborn:

A. LEO is so carefree; he/she does not care if the closets are out of order.

B. LEO does not argue with his/her mother insisting he/she pay the restaurant bill instead of his/her mother.

C. LEO does not think criminals should pay for crimes committed.

D. LEO does not think it is important to win an argument.

E. None of the above.

If you selected E, none of the above, you are absolutely correct. All of the selections except E are examples of LEO being stubborn. Let's examine:

A. If the closet is out of order, LEO cannot find items conveniently; then LEO will complain, complain, and complain until you agree to help find the items. Even though LEO expects a magic hand to throw the items he/she is thinking of out of the closet to them, LEO will probably accept you rearranging so as to make LEO's life easier. However, please note, if you establish a specific place for a specific item, the item may never be moved to a different location in the closet area ever again because this will confuse LEO. LEO will insist the item be returned to the original location and if not he/she will rearrange everything you arrange so the item is where LEO wants it to be, regardless of how many times you move or relocate "said" item.

B. LEO may inherit a "stubborn" gene from his/her mother. Beware, if you go to a restaurant with LEO and his/her mother; you may be waiting to pay the bill much longer than it took to eat the meal because LEO wants to pay and mother-in-law insists she pay. Be prepared to do dishes during the argument and then perhaps the restaurant won't care when you walk out and leave LEO and his/her mother still arguing over who "gets" to pay the bill. (Also, be prepared. Neither one will notice you are gone because they are so involved in the dispute.)

C. All LEOs will say, "Don't do the crime if you can't do the time." LEO's pet peeve is when criminals get away with a crime simply because the courts choose not to prosecute or slick-talking attorneys find loopholes in the laws. It is LEO's devotion and dedication to the safety of others that provokes LEO's strong disappointment when criminals go free or have hardly any consequences. LEO's dedication and stubbornness is why criminals get caught. If LEO knows there is criminal activity, LEO is not going to give up the challenge of finding out who is committing the criminal acts. This stubbornness is why LEO is so admirable in a dangerous, calloused world.

D. If you think LEO isn't stubborn when trying to win an argument, just go back to the restaurant. LEO is *still* arguing with his/her mother over who gets to pay the bill.

LEO may exhibit other little quirky traits you have noticed. For instance, when being seated at a restaurant, LEO likes:

A. To be seated up front so LEO can greet all the patrons coming into the restaurant.

B. To be seated in the back with his/her back against the wall so LEO can evaluate any threats entering the restaurant.

C. To be seated in the middle so LEO can converse with all the patrons at the surrounding tables or booths.

If you guessed B, you are absolutely correct. While most of us do not even notice where we are seated by the hostess, LEOs do. LEOs prefer to sit near the back facing the entrance. I have even heard some LEOs remark how uncomfortable they become if they cannot see who is entering the establishment. To mainstream society, it is no big deal. To LEO, it is a safety issue.

In retrospect, is LEO convenient?

Only if they are able to convince you that eating lunch meat and cheese on a sandwich makes them so.

SLEEPING WITH LEO

Let's examine the sleeping habits of LEO. Between the hours of 10:00 p.m. to 6:00 a.m., most normal people sleep. But as we have established, LEO is not normal. Between these hours, LEO is usually at work, deeply sleeping, dreaming of being at work, or not sleeping at all.

You have probably encountered the Swing Shift Talky Talky. This is the time between 2:00 a.m. and 3:00 a.m. when LEO gets off swing shift and comes home to go to bed. For some reason, while LEO is getting ready for bed, LEO becomes Talky Talky while you are Sleepy Sleepy.

An example: groggily, you hear the back door unlock. LEO is home. LEO stomps through the house to the bedroom where you have been sleeping quite cozily until now. LEO flips on the light; LEO proceeds to take off his gun belt, shoes, uniform shirt, bulletproof vest, undershirt, etc.

After several minutes of delayering, LEO asks in a very loud monotone voice, "Hey, are you asleep?"

By now, even the dead aren't asleep.

You groggily answer, "No, I'm awake." (And so are the dead.)

LEO excitedly tells you, "We caught Naked Butt Bandit tonight."

"That's great, honey," you say muzzy. Then you ask, "Which one is that?"

"He is the one that wears only a black mask. His whole ass is bare, but he makes sure he covers up his face. Anyway, we receive a call of a suspicious subject on Nickel Street at approximately twenty-two hundred hours. Upon arrival, we see the suspect trying to pry open the back door of the residential home in the three hundred block of South Goodman. We proceed to contact the subject with guns drawn because we do not know the extent of his criminal intentions at this time. The only weapon visible on his naked being at this time is the pry bar in his hands. We instruct him to throw down the pry bar and lay prone on the ground. As we surround Naked Butt Bandit, we hear the suspect complain of the sticky pine needles poking his privates. Due to the safety of all, we quickly placed handcuffs on the said suspect."

LEO stops telling the story long enough to climb into bed with you, placing his frozen feet on the back of your once toasty warm legs.

"You are warm," LEO proclaims as he continues with the chain of events. "After placing the perpetrator under arrest and standing him up, I am able to retrieve a blanket out of the trunk of my patrol car to place over the freezing individual. At this point and time, Naked Butt Bandit is cold and embarrassed. The fair citizens of the Goodman neighborhood are congregating, staring at Naked Butt Bandit."

"One senior lady remarked, 'With privates as small as those, he probably doesn't even feel the pine needles.' To everyone's merriment, she continued to sum up Naked Butt Bandit, 'If I had that small of a wink wink, I would cover it up and never show anyone. And just look at the fatty dimples on his butt.'"

"Needless to say, Naked Butt Bandit is very relieved when I place him in the warm patrol unit to transport him to the county jail, handcuffed and blanketed."

Speaking of being warm, you firmly push LEO's cold feet away from your cold legs. As you once again think of drifting off to sleep, LEO decides to proceed to tell you more.

"Then, at approximately midnight, we get a disturbance call in the five hundred block of Dispute Lane. Mr. Maryjane reports that as he returned home from Beerbrawl Bar, he finds a threatening note from his neighbor because of his barking dogs. Upon interviewing Mr. Maryjane, he claims to have the threatening note in his pocket. As he retrieves the threatening note from his front pants pocket, a baggie of marijuana also falls out. We place Mr. Maryjane under arrest for possession of illegal drugs. After proceeding to read the threatening note, we also place his neighbor, Mr. Wanna Killya, under arrest for threatening and intimidating. Although tempted to place both in the same jail cell, upon reflection, the jailer decides separate cells would be best."

And LEO continues to review the swing shift events until you drift off into dreamland, which hopefully doesn't include Naked Butt Bandit.

Let's suppose LEO is working day shift. LEO should sleep as normal people do, shouldn't he/she? No. LEO does not sleep as normal people.

LEO and you go to bed at 10:00 p.m. Suddenly, you are awakened by a familiar sound. Frightened beyond belief, you realize the back door of the house has flung open. In terror, you try to stir LEO.

Frantically shaking LEO, you loudly whisper, "Please get your gun. Wake up! Wake up! Someone has opened the back door."

You stop to listen. You try to hear the location of the possible intruder, but LEO's snores are too loud. You can't hear anything but LEO. You place your hand over LEO's mouth. No good. You pinch LEO's nostrils together. No good. LEO is still in a comatose sleep.

You shake LEO, intent on waking LEO up. "Get your gun. The back door flung open," you insist, shaking LEO frenetically.

Finally, LEO stirs enough to say, "Well get up and shut it."

What? Get up and shut it?

Terrified, you shake yourself out of bed. You grab LEO's gun from the safe place, shaking so bad the gun is twisting back and forth in midair. Focusing on the task at hand, you tiptoe toward the back door, praying you will be quiet enough the intruder will not find you. You also pray LEO will remain sleeping. You fear you will shoot anything wandering about the house at this point.

As you enter the backroom, the wind blows a howling hiss from outside. Even though you are quite satisfied it is just the wind that blew the door open, you peer outside, right and then left. You quickly slam the door shut, locking it as hastily as you can.

You continue to "clear" the rest of the house making sure everything is safe, waving the gun in front of you as if a warning to any unwanted intruder. You finally are convinced it is just the wind. Upon reflection, you also realize LEO forgot to lock the back door. Now, you are *very angry* with LEO. As a matter of fact, you are so angry, you cannot fall back to sleep.

The next morning, LEO doesn't remember the incident at all. He does not recollect any back door opening in the night. LEO slept *good*.

"Sorry, you had a bad night," he says sweetly, winking at you. "I'll remember to lock the door next time."

Somehow, after this night, every time someone comments on how safe you must feel living with LEO, you think of when the back door flew open and you had to "get up and shut it."

Oh, yeah. You feel really *safe* living with LEO.

Sometimes, when LEOs are sleeping at home, they have a tendency of dreaming they are at work. You may have encountered this scenario:

You are sick, sick, sick. You have the absolute worst head and chest cold ever, ever. You wake in the night, LEO sleeping snuggly beside of you. You cannot breathe. Cough, cough, cough. Hack, hack, hack. You need cough syrup. You start to get out of bed to get your cough syrup when all of a sudden LEO lunges for you.

Throwing you back down on the bed, LEO shouts loud, "Don't move! I told you don't move," he warns. LEO is hovering over you with his arms out as if he is holding a gun on you.

What? you think. *Am I just dreaming, or is LEO really standing over me pretending he has a gun?*

Realizing it is not a dream and LEO is really standing over you, you conclude LEO is dreaming he is on the job, apprehending a wanted criminal.

You need to wake LEO up so he quits sleepwalking, talking, or whatever this is.

"LEO, honey, it's me," you say calmly. "I'm just getting some cough syrup. You need to wake up or go to sleep."

For some reason, this sets LEO off. He starts yelling, "Give me your hands! Give me your hands!" as he pokes you in the ribs with his pretend gun.

You find this hysterically funny. You start laughing, which makes you start coughing uncontrollably. LEO reacts by trying to grab you, shouting, "I told you. Give me your hands!" He then starts wrestling you.

Because you are having difficulty breathing, you gently push LEO. The push apparently registers in LEO's subconscious because LEO releases you. He falls softy back in place in bed fast asleep.

Now you are coughing and fatigued from wrestling with LEO.

And LEO? Sleeping like a baby.

Then there is the restless LEO. Perhaps, it is the numerous nights LEO has worked shift work, which requires him/her to be fully alert on duty that gets LEO's system out of balance. Nights LEO can sleep as a normal person, he/she may not be able to do so. LEO may wake up in the middle of the night, restless and seeming to suffer from insomnia. During this time, it is not uncommon to find LEO standing in his/her underwear at 3:00 a.m. in the living room dry-firing his/her duty weapon because of qualifications the next day.

The question you may be pondering is "Do LEO supporters sleep as non-LEO supporters?"

Not if you live with LEO. Not going to happen.

TO REACH THE UNREACHABLE

As LEO climbs the chain of command in law enforcement, it may become harder and harder to reach LEO via cell phone, instant messaging, text messaging, smoke signals, etc. You may experience the following:

You are two hours from home, driving in the big bad city when you experience car trouble. Thinking you are going to cause a major collision at the red light because when the light turns green, your car will not *go*, you decide it is best to try to find the nearest pull off or parking lot. Creeping very slowly into a pull out alongside the very busy, busy street, you manage to gain your wits enough to call LEO for help.

Trembling, you search for your phone. You finally calm down enough to push the buttons to call. The phone rings and rings.

Finally, you hear, "Hi, this is LEO. I am sorry I am unable to answer the phone right now. But if you leave your name, phone number, and a short message, I will get back to you as soon as possible."

You scream hysterically into the cell phone, "Can you come and get me? I am having trouble with the car. I almost caused a wreck at the intersection of Busy and Busier." You plead, "Will you please, please call me back soon?"

Five minutes pass. No call from LEO. Its okay, you think. This has given you enough time to gain back your presence of mind and gulp down all the beverages left in the car. For some reason, this whole thing has made you so thirsty.

Okay, now. Let's try calling LEO again.

The phone rings several times. To your disappointment you hear, "Hi, this is LEO. I am sorry I am unable to answer the phone right now. But if you leave your name, phone number, and a short message, I will get back to you as soon as possible."

"LEO, I am at the pull off of intersection Busy and Busier in the big bad evil city because the car will not accelerate when I press the gas pedal. Do you think you can come help me?" you ask pathetically.

Surely, LEO will be calling you right back. You look around you. Not really in the best part of the city to be out walking around. Oomph. If it looked better, you would walk and get something cold to drink, like some nice cold ice water or a nice cold diet coke. After all, it is about a hundred degrees outside with no air-conditioning. You think it is best not to start the car to run the air-conditioning because this might attract attention you do not want. Plus, if anyone malicious comes too close, as long as there is gas in the car, you may be able to chugalug slowly away or at least run over them if they try to get into the piece of junk you call your car.

As you survey the surroundings, you instantly remember the safety guidelines LEO taught you. You mentally prepare to protect yourself if need be. You crack the windows of the car (not enough for a hand to reach through) for fresh hot smothering air. Now, you are starting to get angry. You are at a deciding point: Are you maddest at the piece of crap car or maddest at LEO for not answering his cell phone? As you ransack the backseat, you find a nice warm bottle of water left from who knows when. You start to look at the bottle of water, pondering, "Wonder who drunk from this last? Wonder if they were sick?"

You don't care. You gulp it down to the very last hot drop.

Your batteries are starting to go down on your cell phone. You know you do not have towing on your insurance and to tow the car will cost an arm and a leg. You will still need to find a ride home, two hours away.

You dial LEO's number *again*.

The phone rings, and stirring your anger even more, you hear, "Hi, this is LEO. I am sorry I am unable to answer the phone right now. But if you leave your name, phone number, and a short message, I will get back to you as soon as possible."

As you overheat, you think if LEO is sorry in his message, wait until later. He is really going to be sorry. Uh-huh!

"LEO, did you get my earlier messages about breaking down in the car in the big evil city?" You scowl into your little cell phone, your lifeline to help. "Are you going to come and help me or not?" you hiss.

You decide to call your son, Vibrant Spirit, who is older now. He should be between college classes. When you explain the situation, Vibrant Spirit assures you sweetly that everything is going to be okay. He is leaving to come and get you. Just sit tight for the next two hours, and he will be there as soon as possible.

You are still so, so thirsty. You look under the passenger's seat and find another old, old bottle of water. Ignoring the greenish growth in the liquid, you decide to drink it anyway. Finally, your thirst is quenched. Don't know what the green stuff is.

An hour passes. No call from LEO. You really need to pee. That green stuff is going right through you. Okay. Don't think about it. Just sit in your piece of junk car and relax.

Great. Here comes Johnny Be Nimble and Johnnie Be Quick looking at you in your car.

What are they looking at? You glare back at them. The two young boys hastily turn to look away. Then, you realize they are as frightened of you as you are of them. You imagine they looked into the hot, sweltering car, saw a wild-eyed frantic woman wet with sweat pouring all over, crimson red from heat and rage, and thought, "Let's get the hell out of here."

You really, really need to pee. Half an hour left until Vibrant Spirit should be here. You are so thankful he is coming to help you.

At last, Vibrant Spirit is here.

Vibrant Spirit is a decent mechanic. He has an idea what should be done and decides to call LEO. He too hears, "Hi, this is LEO. I am sorry I am unable to answer the phone right now. But if you leave your name, phone number, and a short message, I will get back to you as soon as possible."

Vibrant Spirit calls LEO again ten minutes later and hears the same message.

You finally coax Vibrant Spirit into leaving the car, heading toward home, and taking you to the nearest bathroom. (Quick!)

After getting three or four cold, cold drinks for the ride home, Vibrant Spirit and you head toward the house in his truck, leaving your piece of junk car alone in the big evil city. As you get about halfway, LEO calls.

"Sorry, I was in an important, important meeting and just couldn't break loose," LEO apologizes. He vows, "It will never, ever, ever happen again."

The ride home is actually an exceptional time you get to share with Vibrant Spirit. Because Vibrant Spirit has such a busy college schedule, it is nice to visit with him. All in all, it turns out to be a nice day.

You very rarely call LEO, so you lecture LEO time and time again about the importance of answering his cell phone when it is you. Time and time again he agrees it is important, and he will always, always answer it.

The next day, you call LEO to test his new commitment. The phone rings and rings.

Finally, you hear, "Hi, this is LEO. I am sorry I am unable to answer the phone right now. But if you leave your name, phone number, and a short message, I will get back to you as soon as possible."

To which you reply, "This is a test. This is only a test. Had this been a *real* message, you would be instructed as to how to get out of *big*, *big* trouble."

LEO calls back in about five minutes. You smile as you let your phone ring and ring. You know your voice will be saying, "Hi, this is LEO's supporter. Sorry I'm unavailable at the present time. Please leave your name, phone number, and a short message, and I will return your call as soon as possible."

But you have a heart. You push the answer button to talk to LEO about his new commitment.

HOW IT FEELS TO
BE ON PROBATION

You love LEO. Why do you love LEO? Is it because he/she is convenient? Is it because he/she always answers the phone when you call? Is it because you always sleep peacefully with LEO?

Probably, none of the above. You love LEO because he/she is the apple of your eye, the one that hangs the moon, the glitter in your world, the dart on the end of your Taser. You love LEO so much it is hard to understand why everyone doesn't.

There comes a time when it is important to realize not everyone is going to love LEO. In fact, some may barely like him/her. There are others who may actually use the word *dislike* when referring to LEO.

What? You ask with amazement.

And yes, there are even those who claim to hate LEO. What? Hate LEO?

In this world of technology, repeat offenders, such as No Teeth, who LEO arrests frequently may even twitter about the "fucking ass" that keeps throwing her in jail for illicit methamphetamine usage. There may even be rhetoricals on Facebook calling LEO a "son of a bitch, badge-toting prick."

To you, it may be incomprehensible that someone would actually *not* like LEO.

There are also times you may ponder why a media source such as a radio program or local newspaper seems unfair, perhaps even untruthful, in their summations regarding an incident in which LEO is involved.

But the blogs! Woe the blogs. Blogs are made for people who simply have lots and lots of time to write personal opinions about anything, everything, all things they may or may not know about such as police departments, sheriff departments, police officers, deputies, any and all law enforcement entities, any and all law enforcement personnel, any and all LEO personnel matters, events, stories, cases, etc.

If you are a LEO supporter, you may think *blog* stands for:

Believe
Little
Of
Gripers

As a LEO supporter, you may not find it uncommon to read very derogatory remarks about your sweet LEO. What should you do?

A. Respond back to the blog griper calling them a "needle dick butt fucker."

B. Ignore the blogs because you have better things to do with your time.

C. Write an editorial revealing a spicy rumor surrounding a member on the newspaper staff Mrs. Noseytoot told you.

D. Write a blog agreeing with the blogger because LEO never has answered his cell phone.

While response A has probably crossed your mind a time or two, response B is the correct answer.

You read a local article in the paper, which is very negative toward your LEO, even calling LEO "as toxic as nuclear waste." When LEO comes home from work, you proceed to show LEO the article. You rant and rave like a mad person expressing how you are going to respond with a nasty, nasty letter. LEO will tell you:

A. To go for it and LEO agrees to sign his/ her name.

B. Add a few more derogatives expressing feelings for LEO.

C. You are being placed on "Media Probation," forbidden to respond to *anything* because LEO and you are not going to stoop to the same low down level.

D. Start your own local newspaper printing untruths about anyone and everyone who has blogged or written something you don't like.

If you guessed C, you are absolutely correct. You may find yourself being placed on "Media Probation." Speaking as someone who has been placed on "Media

Probation," it is sometimes very, very hard to remain silent. However, in the long sequence of LEO's career, it is better for you to try to ignore matters such as these, recognizing the source from which the criticism comes is not one of merit.

LEOs are usually very strong individuals with the perception the world is not and will not always love them. LEOs only care that you do.

DRESSING THE HOMELESS

His eyes are restless and fatigued. The growth on his unshaven face indicates he has not cared to shave. A black oil-stained ball cap rests on his unwashed head, stained and soiled with dirt, mechanic oil, and grease from previous days. His shirt is pathetically dirty and torn and so are his oversized pants held tight with a tattered belt. Holes are obvious in the toes of the black leather shoes, which at one point in time were of better quality.

As you walk near him in the home improvement store, you hear a geriatric little woman remark to her husband, "I think that is the chief of police."

Her husband obviously embarrassed over his wife's remark, sternly corrects her, "That is *not* the chief of police. Sometimes I don't know how you get so confused."

You smile. You know the truth.

Some LEOs are very particular in regards to appearance, even on days off. However, as LEO climbs the career ladder, LEO may become tempted to dress very sloppy as to ward off those who may want to approach him/her about "work" related issues during their time off.

You preach to LEO about how walking around with him in this beaten-down homeless attire is awkward. People still recognize LEO. It is not as if LEO can hide who he is. It just appears LEO does not have good personal hygiene.

LEO sees this as a challenge. The more you nag, the more LEO becomes convinced he is incognito wearing this pathetic attire.

And to prove you wrong, LEO wears nice clothes into Walmart. After *absolutely* everyone has approached Chief LEO about one thing or another, you finally emerge from the store a couple hours later with a gallon of milk.

LEO proudly puts on his "homeless" wear and insists you accompany him once again to Walmart. Hesitantly, you do, wondering what you should wear. Should you try to find a "homeless" getup to match his or what? And you just pray and pray you do not see anyone you know for fear a collection jar will be placed for you and LEO at the registers in the front of the store.

You trail behind LEO as far as you can in the store, hoping people do not recognize him. To his satisfaction, even people who do recognize him barely wave, apparently embarrassed by his appearance as well.

One long-time friend whispers discreetly, "Hey, LEO, are you working undercover? I'm not ignoring you. I just don't want to blow your cover."

As you walk from the store, pushing a cart full of groceries, LEO proves his point.

"Only thirty minutes and look at all the groceries we got," he gloats.

How do you overcome this tendency of LEO's?

One day, you plan to visit Sunflower Blossom who is an adult now with a house of her own. She directs you in advance.

"Mom, make sure Dad has clean clothes."

"I'll try," you say doubtfully.

She states, "When we were growing up, he would have *died* if we had left the house looking like he does."

"I know. I know," you agree.

One day, as you are standing with "homeless" LEO on the sidewalk of the home improvement center, an unfortunate character approaches. Dirt-stained clothes and ragged shoes dress the poor chap. As he smiles, black space protrudes where teeth have once been.

He hands LEO a five-dollar bill and wishes him better luck. LEO doesn't know how to respond. Surprised, LEO realizes even the homeless thinks he is homeless.

LEO gives the money back.

Thinking this could be a breakthrough to your dilemma, you keep saying over and over to LEO, "See, even the homeless thinks you are homeless."

Does this bother LEO? *Not!* Next trip to town, you look at LEO:

His eyes are restless and fatigued. The growth on his unshaven face indicates he has not cared to shave. A black oil-stained ball cap rests on his unwashed head, stained and soiled with dirt, mechanic oil, and grease from previous days. His shirt is pathetically dirty and torn and so are his oversized pants held tight with a tattered belt. Holes are obvious in the toes of the black leather shoes which at one point in time were of better quality.

Do you think this is part of the law enforcement syndrome *stubborn* trait?

LEO SUNFLOWER BLOSSOM
A.K.A. LITTLE SPROUT

So you think you raised "normal" kids?
You think you did. Or did you?

Scientifically, the hereditary traits of LEO probably need to be studied to see if in fact the law enforcement syndrome can be inherited at birth by the dominant gene of the LEO. It may be your thought that your genes are dominant, therefore, producing "normal" offspring. However, beware that genetically the law enforcement syndrome may be passed down to your children.

For example, when Sunflower Blossom tells you she is majoring in criminal justice at ASU, you think it is a very versatile degree that will serve her well in whatever career she chooses. The thought of your sweet baby girl, Little Sprout a.k.a. Sunflower Blossom, becoming a law enforcement officer does not even cross your mind. If memory serves you well, you believe she confided in you multiple times in her adolescence that she would never, ever become a LEO.

As she graduates from ASU, you cry. You do not know what Sunflower Blossom's future holds, but you are so very, very proud of her accomplishments in college. Now, you must watch as she takes flight from the nest into the *big bad* world.

Then, she drops the *bomb*. She tells you she is seeking a career in *law enforcement*. *What?* You ask several times. Surely, your hearing is amiss from the explosion in your brain.

It occurs to you your daughter won't just be flying into the *big bad* world; she is going to try to land right smack in the middle of it. And you pray.

After pleading, crying, begging, and begging and pleading (did I mention crying?), you finally accept the realization, Sunflower Blossom intends to follow in her dad's shiny boot prints. You aren't sure how this concept happened, but you understand this is her dream, her calling, her determination. You respect and admire her ambition; you know it is in her blood.

She passes all the requirements necessary to attend the law enforcement academy with great effort and perseverance. And you are proud. She talks incessantly of catching the criminal element of society to make the world safer for all, she leaves extra bullets lying in the floorboard of her truck, she buys loads and loads of black shoe polish, and she spends hours polishing her gun and brass.

Wow. Déjà vu. You have been here before.

While a law enforcement academy is grueling and difficult for most males, females may have even bigger hurdles to cross if they are petite in nature. Proving they are physically capable of protecting themselves and others when confronted by a gorilla male may be demanding during defensive tactics. Simple tasks such as finding room for all the necessary equipment: their gun, Taser, handcuffs, ammunition magazines, radio holder, flashlight, etc., on their smaller-size gun belt may become challenging. However, one must always, always remember: It is not the size of the dog in the fight, it is the size of the fight in the dog. Women LEOs prove this daily and should be commended for their valor, courage, and bravery.

How do you feel when she graduates the law enforcement academy? Very, very proud. The hurdles she has mastered in order to graduate are astronomical. As she stands in uniform, proud and straight, with shiny, shiny boots, tears well up in your eyes. Your baby girl, Little Sprout a.k.a. Sunflower Blossom, is a certified law enforcement officer. You look at her new shiny badge. Her courageous stature says she is ready to do her very best; she pledges to uphold the laws of the land. You look at Dad LEO. He too is beaming with pride. This moment stands still in time; one to be cherished and treasured. You fight back the urge to cry, cry, cry.

And you pray for her just as you did for her dad when he graduated from the law enforcement academy. For you, this day is a day of infamy. You will no longer live with one LEO, but two. Thus, begins her journey into a trail of a career with ups and downs, mountains and valleys, and tears and laughter. Since you now have two LEOs in the family, and you possess an extra, extra good sense of humor, your two LEOs will provide you many laughs but not without sacrifices, tears, and an occasional emotional meltdown times two.

For example, you think it is just an ordinary day for LEO Sunflower Blossom and decide to call her to catch up on the daily general topics. She answers her phone as she normally does.

But you hear something in the background. What is that in the background? Sounds like a car revving up its engine, you think.

"What are you doing?" you ask puzzled by the noise.

"Running code on Interstate Felon Run trying to catch a semi that's running hot from law enforcement. I'm catching up with him, and when I do catch him, I am going to do a felony stop on that ole boy," she calmly states.

"How fast are you running?" you inquire nervously as you hear the motor wind.

"Fast enough to catch him," she replies. "Gotta go, Mom."

You sweat and pace until you finally hear back from her that she is okay.

"I'm fine," she declares. "When I stopped him at mile marker twenty-two, I proceeded from my patrol vehicle with my shotgun in hand. As I approached the driver's side of the semitruck, the occupant was ordered to get out and lay prone along the highway. The driver proceeded to look at me, decided to comply with my demands, and slowly lowered himself to the ground lying prone as directed with his legs and arms spread apart so I could view his movements. Backup arrived shortly after I had already placed the perpetrator in my patrol car handcuffed."

"Upon the arrival of my backup, the arrestee asked to speak to the arriving officer. When I let him converse with the backup unit, the truck driver nervously expressed he had never been that scared of a woman before. My backup chuckled and congratulated me on a job well done. At this point, I proceeded to take the perpetrator to county for booking where he continued to nervously express to the jailers he had never been so scared of a woman before. The jailers chuckled and congratulated me on a job well done. From the jail, I heard a chortle and the voice of a previous arrestee informing others, 'She got another one.' To which I personally thought, 'Job well done.'"

You make your mama proud! Job well done indeed!

DAD LEO VERSUS LEO SUNFLOWER BLOSSOM

Terror grips you as you notice the car in front of you is not going to be able to stop in time to avoid a collision with the blue truck only inches away. *Bam!* The two vehicles collide, bending metal and breaking taillights.

As you view nervously from the backseat of your vehicle, you cautiously inspect what other damage there could be. Thank God. Looks to be just a very minor fender bender.

LEO Sunflower Blossom is driving and slowly pulls over to safely stop. Dad LEO is the passenger in the front seat.

LEO Sunflower Blossom expresses relief, "Thank goodness, it doesn't look too bad. Looks like only a fender bender. Do you want me to call for help while you go check on the accident?" she asks Dad LEO.

By this time, the occupants of both the vehicles involved in the accident are out in the road conversing with each other. It is apparent there are no injuries, which is a blessing.

Dad LEO sees the occupants of the collision are just fine and tells LEO Sunflower Blossom that he will call for help while she checks the accident.

"This isn't my jurisdiction, so I think you should be the one to fill out a statement if necessary," she responds.

"Well, this isn't my jurisdiction either, and I think your jurisdiction is closer than mine. I think you should get out and see what you need to put in your statement while I call for help."

This obviously is the outcome when two LEOs have written too many reports lately and do not want another one, even if it is just a witness statement. This is also very interesting because one LEO is just as stubborn as the other.

"I'm on vacation," states LEO Sunflower Blossom, "so you should get out and direct traffic," she directs her dad.

"Well, I'm on vacation too, and I think you should have to direct traffic because you are the one closest to the accident. I will call for help," her dad states.

LEO Sunflower Blossom declares, "I think you should direct traffic because your yellow shirt will show up better than my blue one."

Finally, you have reached your limit. "One of you get out there and direct traffic, *now*," you say, trying to stop the bickering.

Both turn and stare at you.

"Fine, I will go," says LEO Sunflower Blossom.

"No, I will go and direct traffic," challenges Dad LEO.

Both open their car doors simultaneously.

"Did one of you call for help?" you inquire.

"I'll call," confirms Dad LEO.

"I'm already calling," challenges LEO Sunflower Blossom.

Finally, local officers arrive on scene. In the midst of the flashing lights, the responding local officers are grateful for LEO Sunflower Blossom's and Dad LEO's help.

"Thank you both," the responding officer says as he shakes both their hands.

"No problem." LEO Sunflower Blossom smiles.

"Not a problem at all," tops Dad LEO with a huge grin.

Both enter the car simultaneously.

"Thank God no one was hurt," they say at the same time.

"I said it first," says LEO Sunflower Blossom.

"No, I said it first." Dad LEO chuckles.

Competition among the LEOs.

LEO VIBRANT SPIRIT
A.K.A. SMALL TOT

S o you think you raised "normal" kids? You are aware
Sunflower Blossom inherited the law enforcement
syndrome, but you think it is very possible Vibrant
Spirit will be "normal."

Or will he?

Vibrant Spirit informs you of his plan to major in
criminal justice at ASU. You once again believe this is
a very versatile degree, which will serve Vibrant Spirit
well in whatever career path he takes. The thought of
Small Tot, a.k.a. Vibrant Spirit, becoming a LEO at
this time is not apparent to you. You believe Vibrant
Spirit may become a teacher or historian.

What? What are you thinking?

As Vibrant Spirit graduates ASU, you cry
emotionally. You are so very, very proud of his academic
accomplishments. However, you realize his future will
be centered around law enforcement because he has
already applied with a law enforcement agency. He
has already started the preacademy testing process of
the written, physical, psychological, and background

requirements. And he is so, so *excited*. He too is ready to take that flight from the nest and land in the middle of the *big bad* world, plucking up criminals wherever he finds them.

And you think, "How did this happen?"

Vibrant Spirit graduates ASU in May. By August, he is enrolled in the law enforcement academy. He plans to marry in October, in the midst of the academy, and will graduate from the law enforcement academy in December before the year is up.

Your mind is spinning so, so fast; all you can think is *wow*.

You acknowledge the fact that your little baby boy, Small Tot, a.k.a. Vibrant Spirit, is determined to follow in his dad's shiny boot prints by becoming a law enforcement officer also. You know all too well it is his dream, his calling, and his determination. You respect and admire his ambitions. You also know it is in his blood.

He passes all the requirements necessary to attend the law enforcement academy with great effort and perseverance. And you are proud. He talks incessantly of catching the criminal element of society to make the world safer for all, he leaves extra bullets lying in the floorboard of his truck, he buys loads and loads of black shoe polish and almost burns the house down showing his dad how to heat the polish for a shinier coating on his boots, and he spends hours and hours polishing his gun and brass.

Wow. Déjà vu times two. You have been here twice before.

In the middle of his law enforcement academy, you are also helping plan his wedding. Small Tot, a.k.a. Vibrant Spirit, is now a grown, mature, intelligent, gallant, and courageous young man who is driving you *crazy* trying to fit everything into his wedding weekend because he will not be able to miss any extra time from the academy for his wedding. Vibrant Spirit and his fiancée agree they do not want to change the wedding date in October; therefore, the wedding will go as planned. The honeymoon will follow once Vibrant Spirit has worked for his law enforcement agency long enough to earn vacation.

The wedding is beautiful. You are very happy for Vibrant Spirit. You are amazed at how Vibrant Spirit has the fortitude to have a big wedding, attend the very demanding police training academy, and never miss a beat in the meanwhile.

Wow.

How do you feel when he graduates the law enforcement academy? Very, very proud. The hurdles he has mastered in order to graduate are astronomical. As he stands in uniform, proud and straight, with shiny, shiny boots, tears well up in your eyes. Your baby son, Small Tot a.k.a. Vibrant Spirit, is a *married* certified law enforcement officer. You look at his new shiny badge. His courageous stature says he is ready to do his very best; he pledges to uphold the laws of the land. As you proudly look at him in his dashing law enforcement uniform, you see his gun belt holds the same equipment as his dad's. He has pepper spray, handcuffs, ammunition magazines, and a Glock handgun for protection of his life and others. And you pray for him, just as you prayed for his dad and his sister.

You look at Dad LEO. He too is beaming with pride. This moment stands still in time; one to be cherished and treasured. You fight back the urge to cry, cry, cry.

For you, this day is a day of infamy. You will no longer live with two LEOs, but *three*. Thus, begins Vibrant Spirit's journey into a trail of a career with ups and downs, mountains and valleys, and tears and laughter. Since you now have *three* LEOs in the family, and you possess an outstanding, *outstanding* sense of humor, your *three* LEOs will provide you many laughs but not without sacrifices, tears, and an occasional emotional meltdown times three.

As your thoughts return to the graduation ceremony, one of the graduating cadet's wife expresses concern over what the future may hold for her and her graduating LEO. Your mother-in-law assures her everything will be just fine. Your mother-in-law points out the fact that your husband, your daughter, and now your son are all three LEOs. And you have survived.

Jokingly, you tell the cadet's wife, you are the only one of the family not toting a gun around.

To your astonishment, your mother-in-law laughs and remarks, "Yes, she does. You just don't see hers."

The cadet's wife looks astonished too.

As you celebrate Vibrant Spirit's accomplishments, you ask, "So you graduated twice this year and got married. What are you going to do next?"

Laughingly, he answers, "Work with Dad."

Life becomes very interesting when Dad LEO works for a police department and LEO Vibrant Spirit works for a sheriff's department within the same jurisdiction, sometimes responding to the very same calls backing each other up.

There may be dispatch calls as such:

The hot tone sounds. "Bank robbery in progress at Thrifty Bank. Repeat bank robbery in progress at Thrifty Bank on Dollar Street and Penny."

The sheriff's dispatch may announce Deputy E as backup on Dollar Street. The police department's dispatch may announce Chief E as command on Penny Street. If there is any miscommunication in the process, the dispatchers may converse as such:

Sheriff's Dispatch may announce: "Officer E is on perimeter at 105 N Dollar Street."

Police Dispatch: "Officer E is posting command on 200 S Penny Street."

Sheriff's Dispatch: "Correction, Officer E has just verified his location and he is on perimeter at 105 N Dollar Street."

Police Dispatch: "Correction, Officer E has just verified he is at 200 S Penny Street with Command Unit."

In unison, the two departments recognize there are two Officer Es: Deputy E and Police Chief E responding to the same bank robbery at Thrifty Bank. Deputy E is in fact stationed as backup on the perimeter at 105 N Dollar Street. Police Chief E is stationed at the Command Unit on 200 S Penny Street.

When the initial apprehension of the call is over, both departments chuckle over the likelihood of the situation. What are the chances?

And you feel exactly the same way. What are the chances?

DAILY LIFE WITH LEOS

As a wife of one LEO and a mother of two, you will probably notice your world is just a little different than others. While many civilians use spare time to check Twitter and Facebook or MySpace, your spare time is used to figure out the complicated schedules of your three LEOs. You may have to make a calendar of schedules and calculate the following:

Dad LEO works 0800 hours to 1700 hours, Monday thru Friday, this week except he has a meeting Tuesday and Thursday nights. No, no. The Tuesday night meeting is cancelled and rescheduled for Friday of next week. Mark that meeting off Tuesday and place on Friday. (That looks a little sloppy.) Then he will need to be early on Wednesday due to a 7:00 a.m. meeting. Did he say he had a special training on Saturday? Better check on that.

Okay, LEO Sunflower Blossom is on a rotating shift, so she will work Tuesday swing shift, Wednesday swing shift, Thursday day shift, and Friday day shift. Or did she change days? Will she be working Wednesday swing shift, Thursday swing shift, Friday swing shift, and Saturday day shift? Okay, let's figure it out. Don't want to call her while she is trying to sleep during the day; that wouldn't be too good. She said she will be on call from 2:00 a.m. to 6:00 a.m. What days did she say she is taking call? Better check on that. That's right. She said she is working Wednesday thru Saturday. Better mark Tuesday off and write it on Saturday. (Tuesday is getting a little messy to read. Oh well.)

LEO Vibrant Spirit is scheduled to work day shift Saturday thru Tuesday, 0800 hours to 1800 hours because he is working four ten-hour shifts. Okay. Whoops. He said he will be going in early at 0600 hours to 1600 hours on Monday and Tuesday. Better make these corrections. (Does anyone have a new calendar? Tuesday is so messed up; it's not readable.) He said he had gun qualifications on Wednesday at 1400 hours, military time. That's 1:00 p.m. Okay. No, that's not right. It's 2:00 p.m. Mark out 1:00 p.m. and put 2:00 p.m. (Can't believe how many mark outs there are in one week.)

The phone is ringing. Oh, it's LEO Vibrant Spirit. What? Change Saturday and Sunday to 0600 hours to 1600 hours instead. Okay. (Time to invest in a wipe board.)

It's the phone ringing again. Oh, it's LEO Sunflower Blossom. "No, honey, your dad isn't home right now. You need to talk to him about the charger on your Taser. Okay, I will let him know. You tried his cell phone and can't get through. I think he is in a meeting. Yes, I will have him call you as soon as I see him."

The cell phone is beeping. Okay, looks like Dad LEO is going to be late for lunch. Better text him to call LEO Sunflower Blossom about the charger for her Taser gun. Maybe he will be able to help her figure out why it isn't taking the full charge. She needs the full charge on that thing if she is required to use it.

LEO Vibrant Spirit is at the door. "Come on in. You can't stay long? You need to know if Dad LEO has any more .45 caliber bullets for your gun because you want to practice. Honey, I don't know where he put them. He may have used them. You tried calling him on his cell phone and couldn't get through. I just got a text, and he is going to be late for lunch. As soon as I see him or talk to him, I will let him know you need practice ammunition."

The cell phone is beeping. LEO Sunflower Blossom text that she figured out the charger for her Taser and to 10-22 (cancel) asking Dad LEO. Okay. Better send a text to Dad LEO to 10-22 concerns over LEO Sunflower Blossom's Taser charger.

Another text message. Must be Dad LEO. No, it's LEO Vibrant Spirit. Great. He found ammo. Need to 10-22 (cancel) asking about the .45 caliber bullets. The text says he tried Dad LEO on his cell phone but couldn't get through to 10-22. Okay.

The phone is ringing. Oh, it's the family friend, Needta Know. "Hi, how are you? Great, we are all just great. Are the people calling you for donations for the police department and sheriff's department real and not a scam? Let me check with Dad LEO and LEO

Vibrant Spirit and get back to you. I will call you back as soon as I talk to one of them."

The phone is ringing again. It's Needta Know again. "The donation people are so persistent, you think they are a scam and told them no. Okay, then. Sounds good. You still want me to ask Dad LEO and LEO Vibrant Spirit. Okay. I will let you know."

The phone is ringing *again*. It's Needta Know again. "Don't worry about asking Dad LEO and LEO Vibrant Spirit about the donation scam because they called you again, and you descriptively told them you *will not donate any money anytime or anywhere to any organization.* Okay. I won't be concerned about asking." (Wonder if the donation scam people will report Needta Know to the police department for threatening and intimidating? Oh well, not your issue.)

The cell phone is beeping. Oh, it's LEO Vibrant Spirit. The text asks does Dad LEO have an ankle holster for an LCP (gun) he isn't using. Don't know. Will try to find out.

The phone rings. It's Dad LEO. The meeting for Thursday got moved up to Tuesday. Why Tuesday? Any other day would be better because Tuesday is too, too messed up on the calendar. *Unreadable!*

The phone rings again. What? Telemarketers wanting a donation for the local police department. (If Dad LEO were here, he might be able to develop a fraud case.) You respond, "I have a good friend, Needta Know." Click. The line goes dead.

WHEN DEATH WINS

The previous chapters in this book focus on the lighter side of living with a law enforcement officer. However, these last chapters are devoted to the sadder aspects of living with one. Life occasionally presents unwanted directions to be conquered—hard for LEO, hard for LEO supporters.

Every day you get caught up in the daily routine of being; sometimes focusing on trivial tiny problems making them into gigantic, unnecessary crises. This is human nature. This may be your nature until faced with the uncertainty of death. Facing death is often what officers are required to do in order to fulfill their dutiful obligations as described in the following:

Midday, the auto is racing out of control on the busy city streets; 911 is called. Officers respond as quickly as possible realizing the young girl behind the wheel is unable to stop or slow the acceleration of the vehicle. The car is estimated to be traveling speeds of fifty-five up to seventy miles an hour in a thirty-five mph speed limit zone. The numerous intersections present a very hazardous condition for all in the vicinity. Within the mile stretch of the busy city, seconds pass in terror. Within a mile and a half, and perhaps a minute and a half, life is changed forever.

As officers race to the intersections of the city to clear the traffic for the uncontrollable car, time is not in their favor. The vehicle is traveling much too fast to be able to stop danger. One and a half minutes. One and a half minutes is all the time needed to change the world everlastingly, not only for these young victims but also for responding law enforcement officers. The young driver is ejected from the vehicle. Two very small children are crushed under the carnage of the rollover. Death has claimed all three.

One officer responding on scene recognizes the vehicle and the occupants. Shaken by grief, he has to maintain control of his emotions in order to react properly to the horrible, horrible accident. A tear rolls down; his sadness is apparent. He bravely musters through his law enforcement training to continue to react—to react to traffic, first responders, bystanders, and the fate of *death*. Choking back his sorrow, he mechanically performs his duty in order to take the necessary steps to clear the wreckage.

But later, the wreckage will not clear away from him. As he lies in bed trying to relax enough for sleep to carry him into a better world, his mind sees the tangled bloodied bodies of the little baby and toddler; lost forever within the time frame of a minute and a half. The twisted, tortured frame of their mother lying lifeless on the ground nearby haunts him over and over. And he cries; he cries for all three.

The officer realizes this is not the first time death has shaken him; he also understands that because of his profession, it will not be the last. Due to the nature of the career, he knows he is expected by society to be tough, maintaining strength and endurance through all circumstances, even circumstances surrounding death; deaths of innocent little kids and their young mother. He faces this time of crisis recounting all the events leading to the horrific collision. In one and a half minutes, it was over. Ninety seconds changed his memory of life forevermore.

Death affects law enforcement officers in many, many ways. Many officers accept the concept that life is a gift never, ever to be taken for granted. Destiny is always a questionable call, so tell your loved ones you love them every single day. Make each day count. Live every moment as if it is your last. Do not fret over small, trivial problems. Count your blessings and laugh with life whenever possible because you never know when the laughter may stop.

As a LEO supporter, how can you help? How do you support a LEO in this time of need? Simply, be there. Be present for him/her. Listen to him/her if he/she feels like talking. If LEO does not feel like talking, hug him/her. A gentle embrace lets them know you care. If LEO needs some time, it is best to let time heal. If LEO feels like praying, pray with LEO. Be there.

After you pray with LEO, take time to pray *for* LEO and all the victims and the victims' family. Pray for strength. Pray for peace. Pray for serenity. Pray for them every day.

OFFICER-INVOLVED SHOOTING

Hot tone alert. Hot tone alert.

"Shots fired. Repeat shots fired," declares the dispatcher, her voice noticeably wavering as the call is dispatched to patrol officers.

LEO's heart begins to race with adrenaline. Just the tone of the dispatcher sends the message of urgency and danger. Lights, sirens, the motor revving with speed; the officer prepares to enter into the dangerous situation with the hopes of saving innocent lives. Apparently, there is no time. There is no time to set up a perimeter. There is no time to set up negotiations with the perpetrator who is brandishing his weapon, proudly, at the convenient store. Miraculously, no one has been injured up to this point. He has fired his weapon multiple times; no one is able to say how many bullets have been discharged.

The crazed gunman rages with indistinguishable phrases. His haggard appearance indicates his frustration has been rampant for hours, perhaps days.

"Drop your weapon! Your hands up! *Now*," screams LEO as nerves race throughout his/her being.

"Now! Do it now!" commands LEO.

The gunman turns in the direction of LEO. He starts staggering in LEO's direction, yelling, laughing, and cursing. He throws his head back with irritation radiating from his person. Angrily, he lunges toward the officer, raising his weapon with the intent of discharging the gun.

Gunfire is exchanged. The gunman lies in the convenient store parking lot, lifeless.

The officer trembles with the acknowledgement of the occurrence. Thankfully, LEO has dodged the bullet of death. The gunman has not.

LEO hears multiple sirens racing toward him/her. LEO hears the dispatcher calling for a Code 4 (Everything okay.) For a few seconds, LEO is paralyzed with the recognition of how close he/she came to being injured or, worse, fatally injured.

Investigators from another agency are called to investigate the scene. LEO is taken to the police station for a full account of what has transpired.

The phone rings loudly interrupting your sleep. It is 2:00 a.m. You hear LEO's voice. LEO is shaken but holding strong.

"I'm okay, but I have been involved in a shooting. I can't tell you any details because it is under investigation per agency policy. Just know: I love you and the kids. I'm not hurt in any way, and the perpetrator did not survive. I don't know when I will be home. I love you."

You are wide awake now. LEO is no longer on the phone. You no longer hear LEO's voice. LEO feels so far away. You hold the phone close to you in disbelief of what LEO has just revealed to you. The world is suddenly surreal. Echoing in your mind, over and over, are LEO's words: "I have been involved in a shooting."

You always thought these things happened to other officers, not your LEO. You try to remember LEO's exact words. Your mind struggles with the possibility LEO is not all right but maintaining a strong exterior. Over and over you hear every decibel of LEO's voice, "I have been involved in a shooting."

Your mind races; you wonder when you will finally see LEO. You know you will be more at ease when you actually see LEO in person to assess his/her well-being.

The phone rings again. It is a dispatcher, a family friend. She asks if you are all right. She reassures you LEO is at the station. LEO is actually "holding up pretty well under the circumstances."

By the time LEO comes home, he/she has been awake for several hours, but LEO cannot sleep. LEO recounts the incident over and over at first verbally. Finally, LEO just sits, thinking quietly.

The phone rings and rings. Family members, neighbors, and fellow officers call to relate their concerns. The support is overwhelming emotionally. LEO cannot divulge any details due to the agency investigation. Some respect this; others still ask questions they know cannot be answered. The phone continues to ring and ring. Finally, it is best to seek a place of solace and solitude for LEO to reflect quietly and pray.

The press gets involved. Untrue accounts of the event are printed and evaluated by the public. By now, LEO and you have come to terms with the initial shock of the "incident." You hold strong together to face whatever the media and the public may say. And you pray.

Because of the police agency policies, the shooting is investigated by an outside law enforcement agency. LEO is questioned for hours and hours by a detective, or detectives, as to every minute detail of the occurrence. The police agency policy also places LEO on administrative leave until the shooting is declared righteous and LEO has been seen by a police psychologist. The police psychologist has to declare LEO mentally capable of returning to duty before LEO is allowed to do so.

The clock ticks slow. Time almost stands still until LEO returns to duty. The hammer of reality strikes your mental reasoning; you are scared for LEO. You are scared LEO will face death again during his/her shift, you are scared LEO will have flashbacks, you are scared of the repercussions of the shooting.

LEO reassures you. LEO has been trained to react when danger lurks, LEO has faced danger before and will face danger again; LEO will do all in his/her power to control the danger, to protect the innocent lives of the public sector, and his/her own life.

Death calls all of us home; we do not have a crystal ball to know when we will pass from this world to the next. When an officer is involved in a shooting, it is a wake-up call to live each day as if it is the last.

As stated earlier, destiny is a questionable call. Make each day count. Cherish time with your love ones; count your blessings. Pray with your family; pray for your family. Pray for LEO, pray for strength, pray for peace, pray for serenity each and every day.

TAPS AND THE LAST CALL

A young life is taken at the hands of the criminal element of society; a young officer deprived of a most precious gift: life.

A lengthy procession of different agency patrol cars, quietly follows a lone black limousine; all flashing lights in recognition of the sad, sad day. The procession of brothers and sisters in class A uniforms represents respect for one of their own called *home*, for the lone black limousine holds a precious cargo, a brother in law enforcement taken from this world too, too early.

As the procession ends at the final resting place of the brother, officers from all over in many different law enforcement uniforms gather around the brother's family with heartbreaking faces. Tears and sniffles of great sadness echo in the cemetery of the last call.

A gun salute in honor of the deceased brother rings out. An American flag in recognition of the young officer's unselfish and dedicated service and devotion to his fellow man is graciously accepted by a young wife in black, mother of his small children. Unimaginable sorrow and disbelief overwhelm the crowd as tears trek down some of the strong, unwavering faces of the uniformed men and women of valor.

The decorated bagpiper steps forth. Solemnly, he plays "Taps." The notes vibrate the melancholy sadness of the brother's passing.

Then, as is customary, the last call comes. The recording of the dispatcher's voice is heard throughout the final peaceful resting place, calling the brother home. Declaring, "This is the last call for Officer Brave. May you rest in peace."

This is a sad day for all. This day will be a reminder to all in the law enforcement career of the tragedies of the profession.

For you, it will be a day you hold dear in your heart; never to forget the bravehearted, chivalrous ones who sacrifice it all so you and others live in a better, less crime-ridden place. This day, this day of great sadness represents the noble and honorable traits of law enforcement officers, which makes them different than the crime-infested world around them; for they are exemplary of what we all should be.

LIFE WITH LEO,
LIVE IN THE MOMENT

In this crazy, crazy world of constant demands, it is so easy to focus on the activities of tomorrow or the depressions of yesterday. It is so easy to habitually focus on a time past or a time in the future instead of living this moment for the joys of the present.

Living with a law enforcement officer is stressful. Worrying can become habitual if you are a LEO supporter, which is neither beneficial for you or LEO.

My recommendation for living with LEO is to live within the moment. Cherish this day. Cherish this present flashing of time; focus on the present instances of joys and perhaps even sorrows. But live in the present time.

Cherish each day as a blessing. Cherish each laugh and giggle. Cherish the happy times, knowing they will make you smile when you get older and cherish the sad times knowing they will make you strong. Open your heart for unpredictable experiences and stretch your patience for changes of inconsistencies.

Pray. Even if you do not believe in a Higher Power, pray. Pray for LEO, pray for yourself, pray for others, pray for strength, pray for peace, and pray for serenity. Pray for the less fortunate, pray for a better world, pray for less crime on our streets, pray for the young people, just pray.

Yet be prepared for the future. Be prepared for the day your three-year-old grandson says, "Grandma, when I grow up, I'm going to catch bad guys just like Mama, Grandpa, and Uncle Vibrant Spirit."

Godspeed.